THE GROWTH OF
COMMUNITY LAND TRUSTS
IN ENGLAND AND EUROPE

A Common Ground Monograph

THE GROWTH OF COMMUNITY LAND TRUSTS IN ENGLAND AND EUROPE

John Emmeus Davis
Line Algoed
María E. Hernández-Torrales
EDITORS

TERRA NOSTRA PRESS
Madison, Wisconsin, USA

TERRA NOSTRA PRESS

Center for Community Land Trust Innovation
3146 Buena Vista Street
Madison, Wisconsin, USA 53704

Illustrations: Bonnie Acker
Book design: Sara DeHaan

Publisher's Cataloging-in-Publication Data

Names: Davis, John Emmeus, editor. | Algoed, Line, editor. | Hernández-Torrales, María E., editor.
Title: The Growth of Community Land Trusts in England and Europe / John Emmeus Davis ; Line Algoed ; María E. Hernández-Torrales, editors.
Series: Common Ground Monographs
Description: Includes bibliographical references. | Madison, WI: Terra Nostra Press, 2021.
Identifiers: Library of Congress Control Number: 2021916270
ISBN: 978-1-7362759-8-6 (paperback) | ISBN: 978-1-7362759-9-3 (ebook)
Subjects: LCSH Land trusts. | Land tenure. | Land use. | Land use, Urban. | Nature conservation. | Landscape protection. | Sustainable development. | Economic development—Environmental aspects. | City planning—Environmental aspects. | Community development. | Urban ecology (Sociology) | BISAC POLITICAL SCIENCE / Public Policy / City Planning & Urban Development | LAW / Housing & Urban Development | BUSINESS & ECONOMICS / Development / Sustainable Development | SOCIAL SCIENCE / Sociology / Urban
Classification: LCC KF736.L3 W49 2021 | DDC 333.2—dc23

This monograph was made possible with financial support from:

The Brussels Capital Region and from the European Regional Development Fund, provided by the Interreg North-West Europe Programme through a project known as "Sustainable Housing for Inclusive and Cohesive Cities" (SHICC). The SHICC project was carried out over a four-year period (2017-2021) by the City of Lille (France); the National CLT Network (UK); the CLTs of London, Brussels and Ghent; the Global Fund for Cities Development (France); And the People (Netherlands); Self-Organised Architecture (Ireland); the Institute for Creative Sustainability (Germany); and South of Scotland Community Housing (Scotland).

RÉGION DE BRUXELLES-CAPITALE
BRUSSELS HOOFDSTEDELIJK GEWEST
BRUSSELS CAPITAL-REGION

Interreg
North-West Europe
SHICC

CONTENTS

FIGURES

Foreword

Elisa Ferreira
EUROPEAN COMMISSIONER FOR
COHESION AND REFORMS

Over the last years, the housing question has risen on the political agenda. People across the entire European Union are facing lack of access to affordable housing, especially in big cities. In addition to the impact of the COVID-19 pandemic crisis, rising costs significantly affect those living on a low income, marginalised and vulnerable households, which further exacerbates persistent social divides and compromises social and spatial cohesion.

For the European Commission, affordable and decent housing is part of the European model of economic, social and territorial cohesion. While the primary responsibility for tackling housing affordability rests in the hands of Member States, the European Union plays a key role in supporting and complementing these efforts, especially through EU cohesion policy. In particular, cohesion policy funds represent an important tool for supporting social housing, both in building and renovating. Moreover, in 2021–2027, housing stands among the services that have to be accessible and affordable, especially for the groups in vulnerable situations. We are achieving this, for example, by supporting greater energy efficiency in social housing, which helps reduce energy poverty. Finally, cohesion policy support for social housing can multiply its impact when embedded into initiatives based on integrated territorial investment, community-led local development or integrated sustainable urban development.

One such project example is the Sustainable Housing for Inclusive and Cohesive Cities (SHICC) project. Co-financed by cohesion policy's Interreg North West Europe programme, it has the potential to help cities — in the programme area and beyond — to tackle the housing affordability crisis, an urgent and pressing challenge that bears not only social, but also important environmental consequences.

This project is a model case of social innovation: learning from existing Community Land Trust (CLT) projects and regulation and connecting them to other such emerging projects in countries where this housing model is less established. The project has already enabled four Community Land Trust pilots in Lille, Brussels, London and Ghent, with 87 housing units; and more than 300 are under study in the cities of Berlin and Amsterdam, and in Scotland and Ireland. By the end of the project, the partners aim to have established a widespread movement of CLTs across the region, to be widely recognised as a mainstream option for housing supply and urban renewal in all countries. They act as long-term stewards of these assets, ensuring they remain permanently affordable. It is due to these reasons that the SHICC project won one of the 2020 *RegioStars* awards, the yearly competition for EU-funded projects organised by the Directorate-General Regional and Urban policy that demonstrate innovative and inclusive approaches to regional development.

CLT projects offer an innovative and economically sustainable way of providing permanently affordable homes, in the absence of new housing supply through traditional housing models. On top of this, they are enabling communities to take back control of their own neighbourhoods and create a better future that works for everyone.

I am pleased that the this model has a natural link with the New European Bauhaus initiative of the European Commission and cohesion policy's support for social innovation and access to housing. It is an example of a collective reflection on how we live together, our values, our heritage, our new ways of life, our common living and workspaces, our experiences. The CLT model contributes to the New European Bauhaus' aim to foster tangible transformations of places and their use towards a more sustainable and inclusive way of living.

I therefore welcome the model's contributions to building strong communities that support the delivery of its visionary objectives over time. I wish this model great success towards a fairer and more cohesive Europe — of which the present collection of project examples is a promising foretaste.

Introduction
On Common Ground

John Emmeus Davis, Line Algoed,
and María E. Hernández-Torrales

Fifty years after the appearance of the first community land trust (CLT) in the United States, CLTs have proliferated. They have been increasing in number and spreading to other parts of the globe. There are now over a dozen different countries where CLTs have already been established or are presently in development.

The growth of CLTs in England and Europe has been especially robust. Over the past two decades, market pressures across the region have relentlessly pushed prices for land and housing beyond the reach of low-income and middle-income families. Problems of affordable housing, social displacement, and degradation of the existing housing stock have become steadily worse. Governments in England and Europe have struggled to provide effective policy responses, prompting NGOs and community activists to seek creative solutions of their own. Looking beyond conventional approaches to housing provision long promoted by the market and the state, many have embraced an innovative strategy for community-led development on community-owned land where privately owned homes remain permanently affordable — the community land trust.

In England, the first CLTs were developed in the early 2000s. On the European continent, the first CLT was established in Brussels in 2012. The first *Organismes de Foncier Solidaire* (OFS), the French version of a CLT, was established in Lille in 2017. The first *Stadtbodenstiftung,* the German name for a CLT, was established in Berlin in 2021.

There are now 327 CLTs up and running in England, with another 200 in various stages of being formed. A National CLT Network, started in 2010, and the gradual establishment of regional support organizations throughout England, known as "umbrella CLTs" or "Enabling Hubs," have helped to spur and to sustain this proliferation in the number of local CLTs. In France, 64 OFS entities have been created and are now being supported by a national association named *Foncier Solidaire France,* incorporated in 2021. In Belgium, new CLTs are emerging in Leuven and in a number of other cities, inspired and informed by the pioneering work of the CLTs in Brussels and Ghent. Interest in community land trusts has been rising in Germany, Ireland, Italy, the Netherlands, Portugal, Scotland, and Spain.

A cross-national partnership funded by the European Union has helped to nurture this growth. "Sustainable Housing for Inclusive and Cohesive Cities" (SHICC) was started in 2017. The initial partners were four urban CLTs in Brussels, Lille, Ghent and London, working together with the National CLT Network of England and Wales and the Global Fund for Cities' Development. They were joined in the final year of the SHICC project by CLT initiatives in Berlin and Amsterdam and by two organisations in Scotland and Ireland: South of Scotland Community Housing and Self-Organised Architecture. This partnership has been enormously effective in raising the profile of CLTs among policymakers and housing activists across North-West Europe, in planting the seeds for new CLTs, and in providing essential resources for CLT projects.

Featured in the present monograph are local, national, and cross-national efforts to grow the CLT movement in this particular part of the world. The monograph's chapters were selected from *On Common Ground: International Perspectives on the Community Land Trust,* a collection of twenty-six original essays published in June 2020 by Terra Nostra Press. In the years since these essays were written, however, there have been significant changes among CLTs in London, Brussels, England, and Europe — and within the networks supporting them. Postscripts have been added to most of the monograph's chapters, therefore, bringing the story of common ground in these cities and countries up to date.

WHAT'S IN A NAME?

Community land trusts are not all alike. Among the hundreds of CLTs that already exist or are presently being planned, there are numerous variations in how these organizations are structured, how their lands are utilized, how development is done, and how the stewardship of housing is operationalized. What is called a "community land trust" can vary greatly from one country to another, even from one community to another within the same country.

The basic features of the modern-day CLT were originally outlined in a seminal book that appeared in 1972. The design for what was called in this book a "new model of land tenure for America" was drawn mostly from New Communities Inc., a rural settlement founded two years earlier by African-American activists in the Civil Rights Movement. They had sought to combine community ownership of land, individual ownership of multi-family and single-family housing, and the cooperative organization of agricultural production. The book's authors drew, too, on a number of historical precedents, including the collectively owned lands of indigenous peoples, the town commons of New England, the moshav ovdim of Israel, the ej*idos* of Mexico, the *Ujamaa Vijijini* of Tanzania, and the *Gramdan* villages of India.

The model described in 1972 also bore a resemblance to the mixed-ownership scheme that Ebenezer Howard had proposed in 1898 for the Garden Cities of England. The houses, stores, orchards, and factories in the new towns he wanted to establish on the outskirts of major cities would be privately owned by individuals, cooperatives, or for-profit businesses, but the underlying land would be owned forever by a nongovernmental organization, created expressly for that purpose. These scattered parcels of land, despite their removal from the speculative market, would be made available for planned development and productive use through long-term ground leases, executed between the nonprofit landowner and myriad individuals who owned buildings or operated enterprises on the leaseholds. Land was to be held and managed on behalf of *all* residents — rich and poor, present and future — enabling a community to direct its own development, to determine its own fate, and to capture for the common good a majority of the gains in land value that society as a whole had helped to create.

To the mixed-ownership model pioneered in England, India, and elsewhere, the visionaries who created New Communities, Inc. — and the reflective practitioners who followed in their wake — added organizational and operational features of their own, turning the model into something different, something new. Community-owned land remained the foundation on which a CLT was to be established, with a private, nonprofit corporation holding and managing scattered parcels of land for the benefit of residents of a particular locale, especially low-income families in need of housing. What got *added* were mechanisms for ensuring that the development done by a CLT would be guided by the community, as would the organization itself. This was not development from above, dictated by a governmental body, a charitable investor, or a benevolent provider of social housing. It was development from below, directed by residents of the community a CLT had been organized to serve. Ownership and empowerment went hand-in-hand.

Added, too, was an operational commitment to the *stewardship* of any lands entrusted to the CLT and of any buildings erected on its lands. Projects pursued by a CLT were designed to ensure that housing, nonresidential buildings, and other land uses would remain continuously affordable, long after development was done.

These distinctive features of ownership, organization, and operation, overlapping and interacting in a dynamic model of place-based development, became known as the "classic" CLT. Almost as soon as nearly everyone came to agree on this particular conception and configuration of the community land trust, however, the model began to be modified in countless ways. Variations arose in every feature of the "classic" CLT, as practitioners in different places adapted it to fit conditions, needs, and priorities in their own communities or to fit customs and laws in their own countries.

Fig. 0.1. The "Classic" CLT

COMMUNITY
(Organization)

LAND
(Ownership)

TRUST
(Operation)

This continuing process of innovation and adaptation has helped the CLT to spread across a disparate international landscape and to thrive in a range of settings. At the same time, the diversity of meanings attached to the model and the variety of ways in which CLTs are structured has introduced a degree of difficulty to the task of explaining exactly what a CLT might be. Today, there is ambiguity — even a dose of controversy — to be found in the description and implementation of every component.

Community. Throughout the world, most organizations that call themselves a CLT are committed to involving a place-based population in their activities, incorporating a participatory ethos into their organization's purposes, practices, and structure. People who live on the CLT's lands and those who live nearby are encouraged to become voting members of the organization. They are recruited to serve on its governing board.[1] They are invited to participate in shaping the uses and projects proposed by the CLT. Development is "community-led," along with the organization that initiates and oversees that development.

Ambiguity enters the picture because of the varying arrangements that CLTs employ in striving to engage and to empower their community. Controversy arises because some CLTs have dispensed with community altogether, causing critics to question whether they should even be considered a "real" CLT. The traditional model's distinctive features of ownership and operation might be present, but residents who are served by the program neither govern nor guide it; that is, "community" is missing from the organizational make-up of the entity doing development. Variations like these create perennial challenges for CLT advocates whenever they try to reach a consensus as to what deserves to be deemed a "community land trust."[2]

Land. The typical CLT is a nonprofit organization that removes land permanently from the marketplace, managing it on behalf of a place-based community while making it available for long-term use by individuals and organizations. Title to the buildings on a CLTs land, either those existing when the CLT acquired the land or those constructed later on, is held individually by any number of parties — homeowners, cooperatives, businesses, gardeners, farmers, etc. The underlying land is leased from the CLT by the buildings' owners.

This mixed-ownership arrangement blurs the legal and conceptual boundary between conventional categories of tenure, where real property is presumed to be one thing or the other. A community land trust messes up this tidy picture, for it is balanced half-way between the two extremes of *individual property*, owned and operated primarily for the purpose of promoting private interests; and *collective property*, owned and operated to promote a common interest. The CLT tilts toward the former in its treatment of buildings. It tilts toward the latter in its treatment of land, making the CLT a first cousin to cooperatives, co-housing, and various forms of communal, collective, and tribal land.

Although a CLT's lands are frequently and fairly characterized as "community-owned" or, in the parlance of the present series of monographs, as "common ground," these landholdings are neither collectively nor cooperatively owned by the people living on them or around them. Title is held exclusively by the CLT. A community land trust is ownership for the common good, not ownership in common.[3]

There are places, however, where the separation of ownership is made difficult (or impossible) by quirks in the property laws of a particular country or by the quibbles of prospective funders. CLTs have sometimes been compelled, therefore, to retain ownership of buildings as well as the land or to relinquish ownership of both, while imposing long-lasting restrictions on the use and affordability of these properties. Another variation has been developed in Puerto Rico, where the Caño Martín Peña CLT holds the underlying land but uses a durable surface rights deed, rather than a ground lease, to provide security of tenure for people who own and occupy houses on the CLT's land. Some of these residents live on sites which their families have inhabited for nearly a hundred years.

Trust. Although "trust" is part of their given name, CLTs have rarely been established as real estate trusts.[4] Most are NGOs — private, nonprofit corporations with a charitable purpose of meeting the needs of populations who are regularly underserved by both the market and the state. "Trust" refers not to how a CLT is organized, but to how it is operated. "Trust" is what a CLT *does* in overseeing the lands and buildings under its care and in performing the duties of stewardship. Foremost among these duties is the preservation of affordability, ensuring long-term access to land and housing for people of modest means and preventing their displacement due to gentrification and other pressures. Stewardship also includes such responsibilities as preventing deferred maintenance in housing and other buildings on the CLT's land and intervening, if necessary, to protect occupants against predatory lending, arbitrary eviction, mortgage foreclosure, and other threats to security of tenure.[5]

Model. The first book to describe the community land trust called it a "new model of land tenure." It has been regularly called a "model" ever since. A number of practitioners and researchers have grown uncomfortable with the term, however. Some object because "model," from their perspective, carries a negative connotation of something experimental, unfinished, unreliable. They point to fifty years of success, saying that the CLT is no longer a working prototype, but a road-tested, high-performing vehicle that has gone the distance and proven its effectiveness under challenging conditions.

Others object because "model" seems to imply there is only one "proper" way of structuring a CLT, when the reality unfolding around the world is the emergence of many different structures and strategies. Each country and community is composing its own variation on the theme of CLT classic. "Model" tends to be especially problematic for organizers in the Global South, for whom the term is tainted with a whiff of Yankee arrogance, as if there exists some universal blueprint for building a CLT, indelibly stamped with "Made in America." Most organizers outside of the Global North tend to avoid the term, therefore, preferring to describe the CLT as a mechanism, instrument, or tool.

On the other hand, there are still many practitioners and researchers for whom "model" remains their term of choice. It holds for them a positive, prescriptive message of a design, pattern, or practice that is exemplary and worthy of consideration by anyone involved with affordable housing or community development. They are unconcerned that "model" may also suggest that the CLT is still being fine-tuned, still in a state of flux. After all, a restless search for better ways of configuring and combining ownership, organization, and operation is part of the reason that CLTs have been able to thrive in so many political and economic environments, some of which were initially hostile to their germination.

A few of the contributors to the present monograph have continued the custom of referring to the CLT as a "model," but we have not discouraged contributors who have preferred to call it something else. Even authors who regularly refer to the CLT as a "model" also describe it, on occasion, as a strategy, platform, mechanism, vehicle, construct, or tool — sometimes within the same essay. These terms are used interchangeably throughout the monograph.

WHAT'S SHARED?

While there is a lack of conceptual uniformity in the current collection of essays, when it comes to describing what a CLT is or does, commonalities do exist. What unites CLT practitioners and scholars across the world is more important than what separates them. Woven throughout the monograph's chapters are recurring themes that provide something of a *lingua franca* for understanding what it means for an organization to be a CLT and to behave like one. Thus there is a shared commitment to reinventing and repurposing real estate for the common good. There is a shared conviction that community-owned land, in particular, is likely to do a better job of promoting equitable and sustainable development than land that is commodified and owned individually, especially in neighborhoods populated by groups who have long been disadvantaged and disempowered.

Another trait that is shared by most CLT scholars and practitioners is a conviction that the whole of a CLT is greater than the sum of its parts. Across the diverse landscape of CLTs, ownership, organization, and operation are not configured exactly the same in every city and country. Wherever this strategy has been adopted, however, there is a general recognition that it takes more than a single component to make a CLT; it takes more than the reinvention of any one of them to bend the arc of development toward a fairer distribution of property and power. Community-owned land, by itself, is not enough. Community-led development is not enough. Permanently affordable housing is not enough. It is their *combination* that gives a CLT its distinctive identity and transformative potential.[6]

To be sure, there are places in the world where CLTs have been effective without adopting every feature of the "classic" CLT. That model is no longer a template, but it remains a touchstone. It is where most people start, when striving to adapt this complex form of tenure to their own situations. It is where most people hope a CLT will lead, when envisioning a better outcome from their arduous, virtuous labors, whether providing affordable housing, rebuilding residential neighborhoods, or preserving productive lands and local enterprises at risk of being lost to market pressures.

When land is owned for the common good of a place-based community, present and future; when development is done by an organization that is a creature of that community, rooted in it, accountable to it, and guided by it; when stewardship is deliberate, diligent, and durable . . . justice is more likely to be achieved. And more likely to last. That is the moral impetus and lofty promise of common ground.

Notes

1. Organizationally, the model promoted by the Institute for Community Economics during the 1980s had an open membership and a three-part board, representing the interests of the people who live on the CLT's land, people who live within the CLT's service area, and institutions that served that geography, including government, churches, banks, businesses, and other NGOs. See Institute for Community Economics, *The Community Land Trust Handbook* (Emmaus PA: Rodale Press, 1982).

2. To a certain degree, we have sidestepped this definitional debate in the present volume by featuring a number of organizations that self-identify as a community land trust, even if they do not exhibit every feature of what is known in the USA as the "classic" CLT. Our ecumenical embrace had limits, however. We admitted to the company of CLTs only organizations that were committed to removing land permanently from the stream of commerce, placing it under the ownership or control of a designated nonmarket entity and stewarding that land for the common good.

3. This echoes the earliest description of the CLT: "The community land trust is not primarily concerned with common ownership. Rather, its concern is ownership for the common good, which may or may not be combined with common ownership." Swann et al (1972), op cit., page 1. Although the people living on a CLT's land do not hold title

to the underlying land, the resale formula used by some CLTs does provide for a modest increase in the homeowner's equity if the land has appreciated in value during the home-owner's tenure.

4. Trusts are established by individuals to control the distribution of their property, either during the individuals' lifetimes or after their death. Property is often real estate, but it can also be stocks, bonds, or other income-generating assets. The person who creates the trust is called the "settlor." The person who holds the property for another's behalf is the "trustee." The latter takes title to the property (although, under a "revocable trust," the settlor may later reclaim ownership). Proceeds from the trust are distributed by the trustee to a specific list of beneficiaries named by the settlor when the trust was established.

5. Some CLTs are focused less on the provision of housing, however, than on the preservation of watersheds, woodlands, or agricultural lands, either in rural or urban areas. The stewardship responsibilities of a CLT entrusted with managing such lands can look very different than the stewardship that is needed when affordable housing is a CLT's operational focus.

6. The synergy that comes from combining the components of a CLT is explored in greater detail in John Emmeus Davis, "Better Together: The Challenging, Transformative Complexity of Community, Land, and Trust." Chapter 26 in J. Davis, L. Algoed and M. Hernández-Torrales (eds.), *On Common Ground: International Perspectives on the Community Land Trust* (Madison WI: Terra Nostra Press, 2020).

1.

The Once and Future Garden City

Yves Cabannes and Philip Ross

Over 100 years ago, Ebenezer Howard set out on an intellectual journey to define what would make a Garden City. The result, in 1898, was his book *Garden Cities of To-Morrow — A Peaceful Path to Real Reform*. It was written in an age when the memory of the Paris Commune was still fresh, when Marxism was still being formulated, when imperial Europe was at its zenith, and when a young Lenin was still in a reflective mood. It was written in the shadow of the co-operative movement which showed that people were capable of coming together to build their own institutions. In the late 1800s, there were around 27,000 registered mutual societies.

The book led to the founding of Letchworth Garden City, the world's first Garden City. Howard had been reflecting on the industrialisation process that was still under-way in Britain at the time. He aimed to bring the best of town and country together in the ideal town. In Howard's vision, the citizen would be King and the ills of the time — landlords, squalor, pollution and poverty — would be tackled and beaten.

Printed word became reality when funding was found to purchase a large parcel of land on which to build this new town. As Letchworth took shape, inspiring architecture was a key component and the layout of the town was planned with simple rules that reflected common sense. For example, factories were placed in the east so the smoke didn't blow over the town. The architects were inspired by the Arts and Crafts Movement and driven by a belief in green spaces, a healthy environment, and a sympathetic layout.[1] These were the watchwords guiding this new utopia.

However, Howard and his supporters knew that there was more to a good commu-nity and a vibrant town than a carefully designed site plan and attractive architecture. The social aspects would be of equal importance, with ownership and citizenship the key ingredients. A Garden City was designed to be just and fair for the people who would live there. At its heart was the radical proposition of the common ownership of land. This was

Fig. 1.1. Letchworth today, still alive and beautiful. YVES CABANNES

important because the Garden City needed to be more than a well-meaning attempt to build affordable homes. Although Howard may have articulated it differently, the Garden City needed to be sustainable in the longer term. It needed to be economically sustainable in its own right, which is why the capture of rising land values was crucial. Community-owned land was needed if the Garden City was to be socially sustainable and to maintain a balance of affordability as land values rose. The Garden City also needed to be ecologically sustainable in terms of its impact on the environment. Planning played a part here, as did local food production, which was built into the heart of the model. But underlying it all was the notion that the Garden City should own itself.

Letchworth's socialist architects, Barry Parker and Raymond Unwin, were soon helping to design the Hampstead Garden suburb and other areas in the UK, including Welwyn Garden City in England, built on a grander scale than Letchworth. The Garden City Movement quickly crossed the English Channel and inspired Cités Jardins in the Coal Mining Region of Northern France as early as 1905, and new towns around Brussels just after the First World War. Garden Cities appeared around Paris, as well as in Germany, Switzerland, Portugal, and The Netherlands. There were also a number established around Moscow, a result of Howard's book having been translated into Russian as early as 1912, inspiring Russian city planners before and after the 1917 Bolshevik Revolution.

Garden Cities and Garden Neighbourhoods soon expanded beyond the European borders. They appeared in Cairo, Buenos Aires, and Santiago to name a few. Brazil deserves a special mention since Barry Parker, one of the principal planners of Letchworth, advised the City of São Paulo in establishing the Jardim America development between 1917 and 1919. This was the starting point for a significant number of Garden Neighbourhoods and Garden Cities throughout Brazil — more than 45 of them. The concept of Garden Cities also influenced planning in North America. Three Greenbelt towns built during the 1930s — Greendale, Wisconsin; Greenhills, Ohio; and Greenbelt, Maryland — are among the most iconic examples.[2]

It is now more than 110 years since the founding of the first Garden City. With all this history and experience of town design, community development, and various applications of the Garden City model, it is time to ask what lessons can be learned. What should the principles of a 21st Century Garden City be? We believe that many of Howard's original instincts were correct, but how can his vision for the Garden City be delivered in a modern setting?

GUIDING PRINCIPLES OF A GARDEN CITY

The place to start is with a declaration that a Garden City is a fair, just, and harmonious community. It should be a place that is economically, socially and ecologically sustainable. It is not restricted to new cities or towns, even to those that were built following traditional Garden City town planning, architectural, or design principles. A Garden City is about community, not merely about architecture and urban design. It is about building a harmonious community, balancing and combining the best of town and country to create a community where the measure of success is ultimately the happiness of the people who live in it.

As described in a "manifesto" we published in 2014, there are twelve principles that we believe underlie a Garden City in the 21st Century.[3] They are inspired by Howard's ideas, by the legacy of Letchworth, and by successful international practice. We declare that any town or city or neighbourhood can be considered a Garden City if it embraces the following principles:

* Residents are citizens.

* The Garden City owns itself.

* The Garden City is energy efficient and carbon neutral.

* The Garden City provides access to land for living and working to all.

* Fair Trade principles are practised.

* Prosperity is shared.

* All citizens are equal, all citizens are different.

* There is fair representation and direct democracy.

* Garden Cities are produced through participatory planning and design methods.

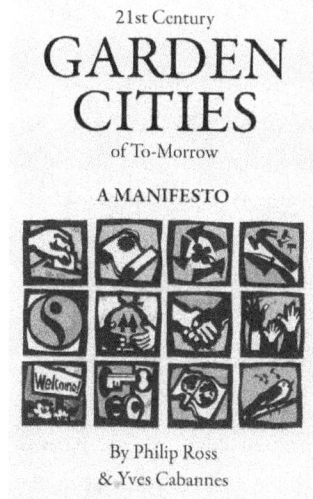

21st Century
GARDEN
CITIES
of To-Morrow

A MANIFESTO

By Philip Ross
& Yves Cabannes

Fig. 1.2. Cover of the 2014 "Manifesto." Earlier editions appeared in 2012 and 2013.

- A City of Rights builds and defends the Right to the City.

- Knowledge is held in common, shared and enhanced.

- Wealth and harmony are measured by happiness.

These principles represent multiple doorways into the Garden City. You can enter using any of them, but deny or contradict any one of them and they become exits. Let's concentrate, however, on the principle that is most relevant to community land trusts: "the Garden City owns itself." That doesn't mean that CLTs do not also strive to put the other principles into practice. But land that is owned and managed for the common good is the main intersection between the Garden City and the CLT.

THE GARDEN CITY OWNS ITSELF

The Garden City is ultimately owned by its local community and not by a series of landlords. This ownership and governance is derived from the people who live and work in the city and who are its citizens acting for the common good. If the Garden City is its own landlord, then it is answerable to and controlled by its citizens, ideally as a community land trust managed by democratic structures that make it both inclusive and accountable.

This principle is the most powerful of all because it is a tangible realisation of citizenship. It is about the real and tangible ownership of the Garden City. It is about common and collective forms of tenure of the city and citizen control of the assets within it. Ownership itself isn't enough, however. There must also be participation: active citizens who are capable of holding the landowner to account. Otherwise the Garden City will not work.

We believe that if people who live in a city have a stake in its prosperity, that will help to engender the idea of citizenship. This is what Ebenezer Howard understood when he envisaged the first Garden City. The Garden City was not to be a charity or something held benignly in trust; it was to have common ownership. Nor was it about people holding just passive paper-shares in the city, speculating on its success, but instead participating in it, building it, making it an "oeuvre d'art"—making it a masterpiece, sharing in its success, and shouldering its responsibilities as well.

The owner of the city's landed assets — or the owner of land underlying a neighborhood — isn't a distant landlord, nor is it the local city council or central government. Nominally, the assets might be placed under the control of the "local council," but in the UK at least, people wouldn't have confidence that the council would defend or protect those assets. For instance, many people believe that if the assets in Letchworth had been placed under control of the district council, they would have been sold off piecemeal over the years to fund lower taxes and to gain political favour with voters. Instead, by locking the assets inside of a trust, Letchworth's lands have been kept together for the long-term benefit of the community —"in perpetuity," as community land trust slogans usually say.

Garden Cities are more than just housing, however. Howard's focus — and ours — encompasses the whole town, not just the housing stock. Agriculture, shops, offices, and other commercial spaces, even industry — anything can be located on land that is owned and operated for the common good.

How can this be done? How can people hold the land in common? There are many ways that residents can be their own landlords. This can be done through a co-operative model, a co-operative land bank, or a community land trust.

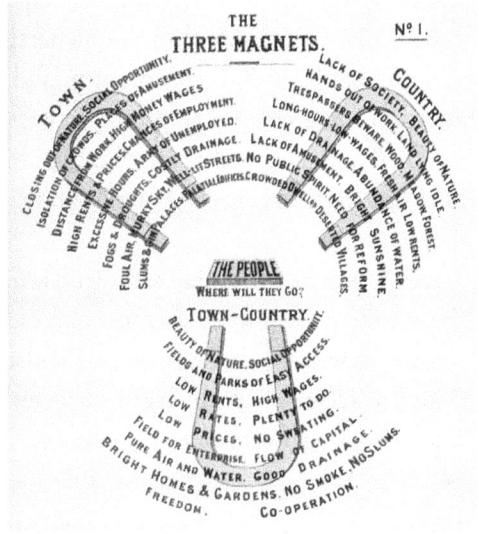

Fig. 1.3. Garden Cities were envisioned to combine the best of town and country, depicted by Howard in his famous image of the "Three Magnets" (right). Letchworth did just that, making land available not only for housing, but for manufacturing (left) and gardening (bottom) as well.
YVES CABANNES

COMMUNITY LAND OWNERSHIP

One of the most successful models of common land ownership is the community land trust (CLT), originated in the United States by Ralph Borsodi and Robert Swann. The prototype for the modern-day community land trust in the USA was formed in 1969 near Albany, Georgia by leaders of the Southern Civil Rights Movement. These CLT pioneers drew upon earlier examples of planned communities on leased land including Howard's Garden Cities, single tax communities in the USA, and Gramdan Villages in India, where wealthy landowners voluntarily gave a percentage of their land, which was then held in trust for lower castes by the entire village.

Basically, a CLT separates the ownership of land from that of any structures that are built on that land. The community land trust retains ownership of the land, whereas houses, commercial buildings, restaurants, etc. sited on that land are sold off, rented out, or owned and managed as cooperatives or for-profit small businesses. We especially like the definition from Diacon, Clarke, and Guimarães on how a CLT works:

> A CLT separates the value of the land from the buildings that stand on it and can be used in a wide range of circumstances to preserve the value of any public and private invest-ment, as well as planning gain and land appreciation for community benefit. Crucially, local residents and businesses are actively involved in planning and delivering affordable local housing, workspace or community facility.[4]

THE UNEARNED INCREMENT

Why bother with this complicated form of ownership? The answer has to do with land values and the fact that they continue to rise. When writing about the revenue of the Gar-den City and how it might be obtained, Ebenezer Howard said the following:

> Thus, while in some parts of London the rent is equal to £30,000 an acre, £4 an acre is an extremely high rent for agricultural land. This enormous difference of rental value is, of course, almost entirely due to the presence in the one case and the absence in the other of a large population; and, as it cannot be attributed to the action of any particular individuals, it is frequently spoken of as the "unearned increment," i.e. unearned by the landlord, though a more correct term would be "collectively earned increment."
>
> The presence of a considerable population thus giving a greatly additional value to the soil, it is obvious that a migration of population on any considerable scale to any par-ticular area will be certainly attended with a corresponding rise in the value of the land to settled upon, and it is also obvious that such increment of value may, with some foresight and pre-arrangement, become the property of the migrating people.
>
> Such foresight and pre-arrangement, never before exercised in an effective manner,

are displayed conspicuously in the case of Garden City, where the land, as we have seen, is vested in trustees, who hold it in trust (after payment of the debentures) for the whole community, so that the entire increment of value gradually created becomes the property of the city, with the effect that though rents may rise, and even rise considerably, such rise in rent will not become the property of private individuals.[5]

Cost and value of land tend to rise, while wages typically increase at a lesser rate, or remain stagnant. Sometimes this land value rises when the taxpayer invests money in improving the local infrastructure, yet it is property owners (and not tenants or leaseholders) who gain the most benefit. The real winners are those who hold a deed to land.[6]

THE CLT AS A VEHICLE FOR CREATING A GARDEN CITY

Despite the prominence given to community-owned land in Howard's vision of the Garden City, as well as in that vision's early implementation at Letchworth and Welwyn, this guiding principle got diluted over time. In many places that called themselves a Garden City, it disappeared altogether. Sadly it was the architectural and design principles that would be copied and celebrated, as architects tried again and again to build the perfect city or town through bricks and mortar alone. Garden Cities became the acceptable face of town and city planning. Its more radical elements, like the common ownership of land, were often left behind.

Community land trusts are a means of restoring community-owned land to the conception and implementation of the Garden City, as well as a means of revitalizing citizenship, another of our twelve principles for creating a Garden City. CLTs are also a way to remove the biggest obstacle to making Garden Cities a reality today. The Garden City envisioned by Howard had a particularly daunting requirement. A group of trustees had to locate and to acquire 6000 acres of vacant land on which to construct a new town accommodating 32,000 residents. That might have been possible in the early half of 20th Century, as dozens of towns, suburbs, and neighbourhoods were being planned and built, incorporating design features that Parker and Unwin had pioneered at Letchworth. That is less likely to be a real possibility today, especially in settled areas of the Global North.

> CLTs insist on the essential conjunction between ownership and citizenship.

We would argue, however, that any town or city or neighbourhood can become a Garden City by embracing the twelve principles we identified earlier, including that a "Garden City owns itself." How does that happen, however, if the likelihood of acquiring thousands of acres of vacant land is remote?

Community land trusts provide a partial answer. They are a vehicle for gradually assembling land and putting Garden City principles into practice — now not later. There

Fig. 1.4. Knowledge sharing, a guiding principle of Garden Cities in the 21st Century. Students visiting Letchworth on a rainy day in 2012. YVES CABANNES

is no reason to wait until thousands of acres are purchased. And land doesn't have to be vacant. Even land with buildings already on it can be brought into a CLT, allowing existing neighbourhoods to be transformed over time into something resembling a Garden City. As John Emmeus Davis wrote in the Postscript to our 2014 Manifesto:

> The promise of the CLT was that Garden City principles could be put into practice right away. Something resembling a Garden City could be created incrementally. It could start small and steadily expand. It could construct new buildings or be woven as a bright thread of rehabilitation and renewal into the gray fabric of a built environment already in place.[7]

Not only do community land trusts allow Garden City activists to get started right away. CLTs also insist on the essential conjunction between ownership and citizenship, as do we. While we extol the virtues of community-owned land, this form of ownership can only be effective if it is accountable. It is by being accountable to the community it serves that a CLT can share its prosperity fairly. Yet this accountability only works if residents are empowered enough to realize that individually and collectively they have the power to question, to scrutinize, and to hold to account those who are operating the CLT.

A community land trust is, by its very nature, accountable to the people who inhabit and surround its lands. It is of the upmost importance, therefore, that the governance and management of the CLT be fair and equitable; otherwise, it can quite easily move from being a socially engaged organization to becoming, at best, a paternalistic one; or become, at worst, a neo-feudal one that exercises control, but is not accountable to its community. A CLT without democratic governance and scrutiny could become the worst of all landlords. A CLT that is dominated by a small group has failed; it is no longer the owner of land of the people, by the people, and for the people.

A community land trust that is economically aware and empowered, one that is socially responsible and driven by those principles, and one that is committed to ecologically sustainable practices is a settlement that is truly ready to pick up the torch for Garden Cities in the 21st Century.

For Howard, it may have been a leap of faith to create a Garden City, but today we know that all the principles of the Garden City have been proven in practice. They have been implemented in settlements across the globe. Individually, each makes a positive impact. But the more of them that we can establish and connect, the greater their impact will be.

The Garden City isn't simply a utopian or idealist vision, but a practical one. It works. It can create a community that is socially, economically and ecologically sustainable. There may be different reasons for choosing a model based on these principles, but at the top of the list is the realization that it will deliver a successful and sustainable community for the long term. To those considering adopting such a model, take courage; you do not stand alone. History, common sense, and a whole movement is ready to stand with you.

Notes

1. The Arts and Crafts Movement began in Britain around 1880 and quickly spread to America, Europe, and Japan. Inspired by the ideas of John Ruskin and William Morris, it advocated a revival of traditional handicrafts, a return to a simpler way of life, and an improvement in the design of ordinary domestic objects.

2. Despite its swift expansion, the worldwide Garden Cities movement became disarrayed with the emergence of the modernist movement and the Athens Charter, signed in the mid-1930s. See: Y. Cabannes and P. Ross, "Food Planning in Garden Cities: The Letchworth Legacy," RUAF Working Papers (Leyden: RUAF Foundation International Network of Resource Centres on Urban Agriculture and Food Security, 2018).

3. Philip Ross and Yves Cabannes, *21st Century Garden Cities of To-Morrow: A Manifesto* (2014).

4. D. Diacon, R. Clarke, and S. Guimarães, S. (eds), *Redefining the Commons: Locking in Value through Community Land Trusts,* Joseph Rowntree Foundation (Coalville: Building and Social Housing Foundation, 2005).

5. Ebenezer Howard, *Garden Cities of To-Morrow* (Available at: *https://www.sacred-texts. com/utopia/gcot/index.htm*).

6. In Letchworth, for example, it is the Trust that owns the land and captures the land's rising value. In 2017, the Trust's tangible assets, made up mostly of lands underlying Letchworth, were reported to have a net asset value of £146 million — which was £12 million more than in 2016 (LGC Heritage Foundation, 2018).

7. J.E. Davis, "A Community Land Trust Perspective on Building the Next Generation of Garden Cities." Pp. 187–197 in Philip Ross and Yves Cabannes, op. cit.

2.

London Community Land Trust
A Story of People, Power, and Perseverance

Dave Smith

Ponti's isn't there anymore. It was a little Italian café which hung from the rafters of Liverpool Street train station — one of London's considerably more perfunctory termini, which sits on the boundary of where the historic City of London meets what is commonly known as the East End.

Ponti's was never particularly famous for very much, although reportedly its full English breakfast and coffee wasn't all that bad. But in 1996 it did star — albeit very briefly — as the setting for a conversation between two of the leading protagonists in a new Hollywood film that was to be called *Mission: Impossible*. So it is rather apt, perhaps, that it was also here, in the late autumn of 2008, that the initial conversation about a potential site for London's first-ever community land trust project took place.

This is the story of that site — St Clements Hospital — and of the people and organisations who, over the next ten years, fought so long and so hard to turn that initial conversation at Ponti's into the permanently affordable CLT homes that stand there today. But whilst it is a good story in many ways, it lacks what is perhaps the key ingredient of any great story: namely, a definitive and happy ending. Not because there haven't been some real highs and lasting achievements within the organisation's first decade — there have been many. But because what has also emerged during this time is the sheer scale and deepening extent of the housing problem, and how desperately the CLT's work is needed. And so it is unlikely that this is a story that will come to an end any time soon.

Today, the London CLT has active campaigns relating to twelve potential further sites across the capital. Based upon its most conservative projections, the organization is now on track to deliver some 110 new permanently affordable homes by 2022. This will see upwards of 300 people living in CLT homes in parts of the city as far apart as Croydon and Redbridge; in places of such historical and cultural significance as Cable Street and Brixton; and maybe even on the Olympic Park. But with over 8,500 people sleeping rough last year, with 365,000 children under the age of 16 still living in accommodations that are legally deemed "overcrowded," and with over 240,000 households still on government waiting lists for affordable housing in one of the wealthiest cities in the world — St Clements was only ever going to be able to be considered a success if it was merely the beginning of a much longer story, laying the foundation for a CLT that could do even more in the future.

AN UNAFFORDABLE CITY—A BRIEF HISTORY

The housing crisis in London (and especially in the city's East End, where the London CLT got its start) is nothing new. Charles Booth — the great Victorian social researcher and reformer — in his famed "Poverty Maps" of 1891, described some of the neighbouring streets around what is now the St Clements site as being typified by the "Very poor, casual. Chronic want."

Where Victorian slums had dominated, post-war governments of all political colours took the opportunity afforded to them by the Luftwaffe to remake vast swathes of the East End following the annihilation of its Docklands between 1939–45. In their place were built large-scale social housing estates — concrete monoliths promising "streets in the sky." Local politicians looked to outbid each other in regards to the number of new homes they promised to build during each election cycle. This interventionist consensus, broadly speaking, remained the case until the end of the 1970s, when Horace Cutler (the Chairman of Housing and, later, Leader of the Conservative party within the Greater London Council), and then Margaret Thatcher, actively sought to curb the ability of local councils to build subsidized public housing in an attempt to reduce their political opponents' power base. The effect was that the overall number of new homes being built in London — and particularly the number of *affordable* homes being built — fell off a cliff edge: down from about 35,000 a year in total in 1969 to fewer than 14,000 a year in 1985. The private sector (thoroughly aware of the impact that a decrease in supply would have on its profitability) never picked up the slack. So prices began to rise in relation to earnings — albeit at a relatively moderate rate at first, as the great legacy of the welfare state clung on and the economic volatility of the 1980s gave way to recession in the early 1990s.

The picture changed, however, in the closing years of the Twentieth Century. With an economic recovery, coupled with the election of a New Labour government in 1997 and a belief in all things "third way," the British housing market embarked upon a record run of unbroken economic growth that would last for fifteen years. These were boom times. One of the nation's largest mortgage lenders, Northern Rock, demutualized to become a bank in the same year. It infamously offered "120% loan-to-value interest-only" mortgages to first-time homebuyers, a sign that both the bank and homebuyers were convinced that the property market would rise indefinitely. As such, borrowers were encouraged to take out a loan for more than a house's value, spend the extra capital on moving and furnishing costs, and plan to never repay the capital sum, believing all the while that they could still make money out of the property's appreciation.

House prices in London rose from an average of £96,000 in 1997 to over £300,000 just ten years later. The global economic crash of 2008 took its toll briefly, but by the summer of 2012 house prices were back to where they had previously been and quickly rose again. As of 2019, the average house price (the geometric mean) across the whole city of eight million people stood at £478,853 ($631,998). This was approximately fourteen times the average Londoner's salary of £34,000 ($44,873) and nearly twice that of the national average house price of £243,583 ($321,485) in a country that is known to have a nationwide housing crisis.

COMMUNITY ORGANIZING AROUND LONDON'S BID TO HOST THE 2012 OLYMPICS

The impact of these macro-economic trends was plain for all to see at street level. In East London, at meetings of The East London Communities Organisation (TELCO) — the country's first and now largest community organising federation, known today as Citizens UK — stories poured forth about the crippling costs of rent and a homeownership market out of reach. Following its earlier transformative success with the Living Wage Campaign, Neil Jameson — TELCO's founding Executive Director, who had trained at the Industrial Areas Foundation in the late 1980s and exported Saul Alinksy's organising model to the UK — decided that housing needed to form a central plank of the organisation's new agenda. And a prime organising opportunity soon appeared in the summer of 2005, thanks to a meeting taking place some six thousand miles away in Singapore.

London had recently declared its intention to bid for host city status for the 2012 Summer Olympic Games. Sensing their chance to leverage influence within a formative political debate — and especially given the desire of the authorities to secure local support for a bid that was premised on a promise of a "legacy"

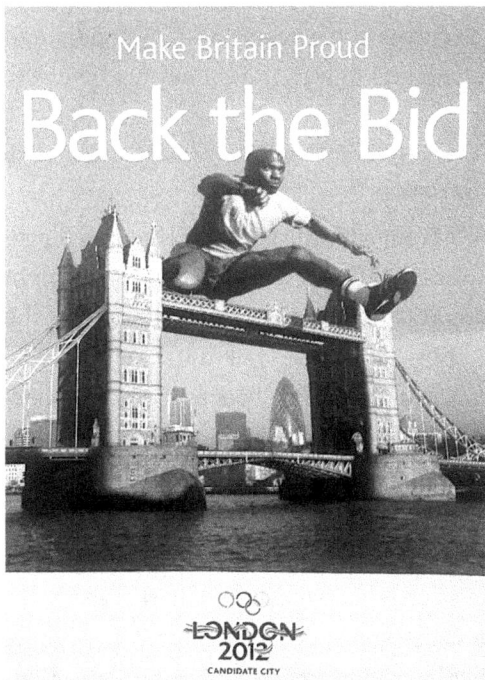

Fig. 2.1. Poster urging London's citizens to support the city's bid to host the 2012 Olympics.

of regeneration for East London, amidst an anticipated total spend of £8.7 billion—TELCO forced itself into a relationship with the London 2012 Bid Team and invited the Team to one of TELCO's public assemblies. Built on a foundation of thousands of one-to-one conversations within trades unions, churches, mosques, schools, and other civic institutions across East London, the result of the organizing effort was the preparation and public signing of an "Ethical Charter for The Games." This agreement guaranteed a defined set of community benefits in exchange for TELCO's support for the Olympic bid. Amongst them was a commitment to new jobs and the payment of a Living Wage for all staff at the Olympics. There was also a commitment to build, once the Games were over, "2012 permanently affordable homes for local people through a Community Land Trust and mutual home ownership."

The announcement by the International Olympic Committee in Singapore on July 6, 2005 that London was to be awarded the right to host the Games of the XXX Olympiad was largely unexpected and met with mixed emotions across the British capital. Paris had been widely expected to win, and many Londoners greeted the news with a combination of stereotypical British disdain and reserve, as well as newfound fears about the implications for where they would be able to park. But for those in TELCO, the mood could not have been happier. The Ethical Charter for The Games had been signed by none other than Lord Sebastien Coe, head of the Bid Team and now the Chairman of the London Organising Committee of the Olympic and Paralympic Games (LOCOG), and by the Mayor of London, Ken Livingstone. That agreement looked set to ensure that London's first CLT was a done deal and headed for rapid success in the years ahead. But sadly, and perhaps inevitably, as so often happens when land and power and money are involved, this was not to be the case.

Broken Promises

Little communication was received from the Bid Team after the announcement in Singapore. The newly formed Olympic Delivery Authority (ODA) then ignored the agreement with TELCO, refused to meet with TELCO's representatives, and even claimed that the Ethical Charter was not their concern, since the ODA had not been in existence when the agreement was signed. Some mild and well-mannered agitation from TELCO followed — including gatherings outside ODA meetings. The Authority responded with a letter in 2006 that stated that, whilst the Charter and commitment to a CLT was still an aspiration, the ODA viewed that agreement as nothing more than a memorandum of general understanding "in principle," subject to "considerations of delivery." As such, after the Games, any highly-prized land at the Olympic Park would be considered for the development of CLT homes only if a "working pilot" could

> Land at Olympic Park would be considered for the development of CLT homes only if a "working pilot" could be established.

be established elsewhere in the city beforehand, as a functioning proof of concept for this unfamiliar model.

What was becoming increasingly clear was that waiting on the Olympic authorities and city officials to deliver London's first CLT was unlikely ever to work, so East London's communities decided to take matters into their own hands. On a bright sunny morning in July 2007, TELCO descended on the land immediately opposite London's City Hall, pitched fifty tents, and refused to move until Mayor Ken Livingstone came out and promised to make some land available for a CLT pilot. After much to-ing and fro-ing — first with his staff and then with the Mayor himself — Livingstone appeared, and pledged that a site would be made available. After snapping some smiling pictures, everyone left, convinced once more that progress towards London's first CLT was being made.

The land that Livingstone eventually proposed, however, was a disused industrial path called Bow Lock on the very eastern edge of the borough of Tower Hamlets: a forgotten space between a main arterial road and the River Lea. The chief problem, however, as TELCO later discovered, was that the land promised by the Mayor was not actually his to gift. Rather than belonging to his office, the land belonged to the local council, which was far less keen on the idea of their land being given away. And so, despite four years of campaigning, come the beginning of 2008, the campaign was back at square one. A new site needed to be found.

The Meeting at Ponti's

It was around this time that the campaign decided it needed to professionalize in terms of its housing expertise, and employ a different organisational structure beyond just the broad-based community organising tactics it had previously utilized. In response to the cry of "Give Us Some Land!," the repost from those in power at the Authority and at City Hall had become clear: "What land? And to Whom? (You expect us to give land to that rabble waving placards?!)."

The East London Citizens Community Land Trust Ltd had been formed in 2007, but up until now it had been just a campaign. Neil Jameson, TELCO's Executive Director, along with Matthew Bolton, the Lead Community Organizer for East London, had long been on the lookout for allies who could help them put a firmer structure in place. Amongst those they discovered was Stephen Hill — a long-established and well-respected housing expert, who after years of working for a number of social housing organisations and public bodies, had taken to doing what he described as "only the interesting and worthwhile work" as a freelance contractor. By chance, he had briefly been employed by the Olympics planners, helping them to run some public workshops around potential uses of the Olympic Park after the Games. It was at one of these meetings — when TELCO had arrived yet again to make a nuisance of themselves — that Stephen quietly mentioned to Neil and Matthew that he was very much "on their side." He offered to meet up afterwards to see if he might help to move things forward.

Around the same time, TELCO appointed its first dedicated Housing Organizer — a twenty-two-year-old named Dave Smith. He had recently returned from a stay in Massachusetts, volunteering on the Obama primary campaign, and was eager to become involved in community organising like that he had read about that was going on in the US. In Neil Jameson's words, he "simply wouldn't leave us alone." This was — by all accounts — Smith's chief, and perhaps only, qualification for being offered the job. Nevertheless, he set about starting to formalize the campaign and to search for a new site. However, given TELCO's limited resources, he could only be paid for one day a week. So the rest of his time was spent keeping bar at a local pub called The Little Driver, at the end of the road where he was living in Bow.

Each Monday, he would walk the mile or so to TELCO's offices in Whitechapel to meet with the formative campaign membership that TELCO had begun to put together, heading along Mile End Road past a disused hospital site called St Clements. His induction to the new job was short — a two-day seminar on Alinsky and organising, and a list of three names of people to meet with. Top of this list was Stephen Hill — who suggested that they meet for coffee at Ponti's Café in the Liverpool Street train station.

THE CAMPAIGN TO ACQUIRE ST CLEMENTS

At that very first meeting, Stephen and Dave discussed the prospect of acquiring the boarded-up St Clement's hospital site as the potential home for London's first CLT. Designed by a renowned architect Richard Tress and constructed in 1849 for £55,000 (a princely sum for that time!), the building had had a succession of occupants and uses over the years. It had originally operated as a workhouse for the poor, with accommodations for 800 inmates. It boasted Siberian marble pillars, a chapel with stained glass, and an elegant Board of Guardians Room for those who oversaw its operations.

As workhouses were phased-out throughout the country, it became the Bow Infirmary in 1874, and was then renamed the Bow Institution in 1912, caring for the long-term sick. The building became a psychiatric unit in 1936 under the new name of St Clement's Hospital. Despite being bombed heavily during the Second World War, it remained a sight to behold, until eventually closing its doors in 2005. Ownership of the land and buildings then reverted from the National Health Service (NHS) to the office of the Mayor of London. The site then sat vacant for years, awaiting its planned sale for private housing development.

Walking along the Mile End Road in 2009, Dave Smith had noticed that the vacant buildings, despite being weathered and derelict, remained architecturally impressive. But from a community organizer's point of view the site was even more special. It straddled almost the exact midpoint of the road running from the center of London to the proposed site for the Olympic Stadium. As he later recalled:

CITY OF LONDON UNION WORKHOUSE.——Mʀ. R. Tʀᴇss, Aʀcʜɪᴛ ᴇcᴛ.

Fig. 2.2. Original design and purpose of the St Clements site, 1849.

It was in the heart of our power base . . . surrounded by our member institutions. And above all else, it had the capacity to take the campaign out of the abstract — away from theory and policy — and root it in a sense of place for families who needed somewhere to call home. They could actually see themselves potentially living there. And from the moment we first set our sights on it, the campaign truly took off.

The newly revitalized campaign group met for the first time on a cold winter's Saturday in November, in a flat overlooking the muddy expanse that was set to become the Olympic Park. The group had identified four potential sites. A vote on which of these to pursue was taken a few weeks later in a second meeting at Bryant Street Methodist Church. But there was never any question of which site was going to win. Unanimously, the campaign group chose St Clements as its target for developing London's first CLT homes.

Soon after, the campaign took another early giant step forward with the arrival on the scene of Chris Brown, Chief Executive of an ethical property developer named "igloo Regeneration." East London CLT had no track record, little direct development expertise, and only just enough money to pay its one-person staff for one day a week. This fledgling organization needed quickly to transform itself to be able to competitively tender for prime real estate worth tens of millions of pounds in one of the UK's hottest housing markets. The newly elected Board — drawn mostly from the community organising base — met with Chris Brown and entered into a partnership with igloo Regeneration.

Over the next year, this highly progressive developer and the CLT's board collaborated in developing both a competitive housing proposal and a high-profile political campaign to win the tender. As soon as Brown's team were on board, architects were appointed, plans were drawn up, financial modelling was commissioned, and the bid to build London's first CLT homes was at last in full motion. The CLT's founding Chairman, Paul Regan, later said: "Few did more in those early days than Chris Brown — and Stephen Hill throughout — to drag our pipe-dream of acquiring St Clements from a well-meaning longshot to a viable proposition."

> The CLT was given a classic lesson in the trials and tribulations of community-led development.

It was also around this time that a talented young architect named Calum Green — who would go on to lead the organisation in the years ahead — joined the staff team. Pioneering the CLT's community-led design work, he and Dave worked together over the three years that followed, as the tender process was drawn out and the East London CLT was given a classic lesson in the trials and tribulations of community-led development. Reluctant bureaucrats at City Hall sought to temper the public commitments made in front of Citizens Assemblies by Mayor Ken Livingstone and, subsequently, by Mayor Boris Johnson. The tender documents were reissued approximately fifteen times. The multinational private developers who were also bidding for the contract set up a pseudo, one-person "CLT" in order to try and win the competition.

Fig. 2.3. St Clements action, circa 2009.

But the East London CLT persisted, continually building their organisation and their political campaign. The CLT worked closely with local civic institutions in Tower Hamlets, including Darul Ummah and the East London Mosque. Students at Queen Mary, University of London, under the tutelage of Professor Jane Wills, studied the site and assembled data that could be used in planning its redevelopment for lower-income families. And the CLT's Vice-Chair, Colin Glen, and his black-majority New Testament Church of God in Mile End, hosted boisterous Annual General Meetings which kept CLT members and the general public both informed and enthused about the campaign.

Compromise on Everything
Except Your Principles and Winning

The eventual outcome of the tender was a political compromise. It was decided by Mayor Boris Johnson that ownership of the St Clements site should go in part to the East London CLT. This was undoubtedly a win for the organization and set it on the path to becoming the largest CLT in the United Kingdom. But, sadly, he also ruled that the East London CLT/igloo Regeneration bid would not win the contract to redevelop the site. Instead, the City awarded the contract to a private developer, Linden Homes. Because of the political stir the CLT had caused, however, including coverage on the front page of the *London Evening Standard*, the selection of Linden Homes was conditional on the developer being able to strike a deal with the East London CLT to integrate a specified number of resale-restricted CLT homes into the new development.

The pressure from City Hall to build a new relationship and to make it work quickly was now on, but so too was the pressure from the local community to strike a deal that stayed true to the CLT's promises and original purpose. An all-member Open Meeting of the East London CLT was thus called in the Methodist Church opposite the St Clement's site to discuss the forthcoming negotiation with the private developer. The CLT would get 23 homes, slightly fewer than it had sought in its original bid. It would also be forced to abandon the relationship with igloo Regeneration and to team up with a developer with whom the East London CLT had no prior relationship in order to deliver a scheme that differed drastically from the CLT's community-led designs. On the other hand, the option on the table was still significant. Andy Schofield, a founding Board Member and later the CLT's Project Director, led the Open Meeting. A hundred people participated in a formal discussion of what they felt "a CLT must be," "a CLT could be," and "a CLT could not be."

Inspired by their community organising training — which draws upon the lessons of Thucydides and the debate between the Athenians and the islanders of Melos — East London CLT members collectively crafted a negotiating position that reflected their priorities:

- The CLT must deliver permanent affordability;

- The St Clement's project should be based-upon principles of community-led design, so the site plans proposed by the developer should be revisited and redrawn; and

- The CLT's homes must not be controlled, managed, or owned by other parties.

With the battle lines drawn, the Board Chair and the Director for the East London CLT headed into their first meeting with executives from Linden Homes in a hotel just opposite Buckingham Palace. The CLT's representatives had a magnificent platform from which to press their case, due to the power of ordinary citizens organizing. Three hours later, with all of the CLT's conditions met, the deal for London's first community land trust project was signed. It was April 2012.

THREE LESSONS FOR CLTs EVERYWHERE

The story goes on from there — through a series of community-led design charrettes and a total redesign of the site plan; through the planning application process; through the financial and contractual negotiations; to the ground-breaking in March 2014, which featured Mayor Boris Johnson happily driving a bulldozer around the site. There were ups and downs along the way, too numerous to tell. But for those of us who went through the whole process — many of whom are still actively involved today, in what has since expanded and so been renamed the London CLT — there have been three lessons within our experience that we believe to be relevant to the CLT movement worldwide.

1. A "Classically" English CLT?

The first is a reflection upon an incredibly important debate: namely, to what extent should the "classic" CLT model — with its history, its proven track record, but also its chiefly American practice and legal construct — be open to interpretation and change in other countries? And how should a new organisation find the appropriate balance between adapting the model to meet local conditions, whilst maintaining a common understanding of the model's features and purpose, among all organisations that wish to call themselves a CLT?

Definitions and explanations of the CLT model in the UK are inherently ambiguous, and intentionally so. When the community land trust was first written into law as part of the Housing and Regeneration Act of 2008, the CLT pioneers who drafted that legislation did so in a manner they believed would allow CLTs to be expansive and innovative. Their proposal was adopted with minimal alteration. As a result, there were no statutory requirements for a CLT to follow the "classic" model, as it had evolved in the United States, nor was there any mention in the law of the necessity of ensuring the permanent affordability. The law said only that a CLT was *"to ensure that the assets are not sold or developed except in a manner which the trust's members think benefits the local community."*

A case could be made that such organizational ambiguity, where a CLT may be organized and operated in many ways, has been essential to the growth and success of CLTs in the UK. The London CLT chose very consciously, however, to adopt many of the traits of the "classic" model. Outward looking, it drew a clear line of distinction between CLTs and established housing associations and co-ops in the UK, which had long provided affordable housing of various types, but which didn't involve the community in the same way.

The result was an organization that is structured as closely to the "classic" CLT as possible within the legal confines of the UK system. In fact, the London CLT follows the American tradition more closely than any other CLT currently established in the UK. This was not without its problems. In many ways, there are tasks that would probably have been more quickly and readily achieved had the organization entirely anglicized its structures. But the organizers, leaders, and members of the London CLT felt that a too drastic departure from the "classic" model would excessively distance themselves from a growing international CLT movement. They felt strongly aligned to that movement, so they wanted to promote a structure and purpose that were consistent with most other CLTs in the world.

The resulting arrangements, at least on paper, can look somewhat messy. The tripartite composition of the London CLT's board does not always resonate immediately with members and needs constant explaining. And leaseholder laws in the UK mean that "owning the land" outright is both far less common and less simple than elsewhere. (London

Fig. 2.4. Board of directors, London Community Land Trust, 2019.

CLT does not own the "freehold" at St Clements in the same way as CLTs elsewhere, but in terms of local property laws this is a technicality rather than a meaningful distinction.)

As such, we have come to conclude, much like John Davis said on one of several visits to the London CLT, that CLT organizers must confront the difficult challenge of finding the right balance between adopting the "classic" model and adapting that model to their own peculiar local and national circumstances, for the sake of balancing practical challenges and maintaining a movement worldwide. Davis went on to say:

> It was absolutely essential for us [in the United States] to develop a common language, a common understanding of what a CLT is. Without that, it was hard to distinguish the CLT from competing models, competing traditions; it was hard to draw people together under the banner of CLTs until there was a common vocabulary. Conversely, once you have agreement as to what a CLT is, it gives you the freedom to innovate within that structure and to improve the "classic" model . . . . But if you modify too much, you risk severing the connection to our roots, to our values, to the sense of purpose and struggle that comes from them. . . . So a common understanding of the model creates a yardstick of values and performance against which you can assess whether a proposed innovation will help or hinder.

2. Linking House Prices to Local Wages to Create True Affordability

The second lesson we learned is the importance of a locally-determined definition of the term "affordable housing." In the UK, following changes made by the national government in 2010, the term "affordable housing" became a source of derision, having been adjudicated in law to mean anything "up to 80% of the open-market rate," which in London is now rarely affordable to anyone. As such, the term has lost all meaning. Yet, in the first instance, the London CLT had planned to devise its sales values in a similar way. The original plan had been to sell fixed, capped-equity shares at approximately 60% of the open-market value. That changed in October 2011, when board members and staff from the London CLT attended the National CLT Conference in the United States.

As part of that conference, after a long boat journey from Seattle to OPAL Community Land Trust in the San Juan Islands, the visitors from London had an in-depth conversation with Lisa Byers, OPAL's Executive Director. Thoughtful and eloquent in her exposition, she extolled the virtues of linking the cost of homes not to any percentage of the open market value — "which we all accept is an inherently broken and an unrelated assessment of what people on local wages can afford"— and tying it instead to a multiplier of average local incomes. This was a transformative moment for the London CLT, for it not only provided a clear mechanism for its stated aim of delivering "truly affordable homes," but also provided the CLT with a unique and compelling narrative for what it was about —"homes that local people on local wages can afford."

Back home, those on the trip crunched the numbers and — after a lot of work with local groups to gut-check the impact of this new resale formula — established their own wholly unique but quite brilliant mechanism by which the homes were to be sold. Prices were to be determined by: (a) taking the median average wage in the area in which the homes were to be built; (b) applying the principle that no family should be forced to spend more than one third of their income on housing; and then (c) multiplying this figure out by a standard set of mortgage assumptions (e.g., 25-years at an average rate of interest and with a 10% downpayment). This calculation yielded a price that local people could genuinely afford to pay — a price that was created by working backward from their own circumstances, rather than being derived from market conditions. If residents ever chose to move, they would be bound to apply the same formula in calculating the resale price of their homes. CLT house prices would always rise in line with wage inflation, therefore, rather than rising in relation to market-driven house and land prices that are increasingly beholden to the whim of foreign investors or buy-to-leave landlords.

> London CLT strives to be not only a social justice campaign, but also the best consumer choice.

The London CLT — which strives to be not only a social justice campaign, but also the best consumer choice available to any median-income household — had found its niche. With three-bedroom houses (including a garden) at St Clements going on sale for £235,000 ($295,000) through the CLT, compared to costs starting at £600,000 ($755,000) for market-rate homes offered next door by the private developer, the London CLT had created a defining, replicable, and sustainable proposition for permanently affordable housing across the city.

3. Keeping Community in the CLT

The third and most important reflection on this journey is that, above all else, community land trusts must "keep the C in CLT." It is this, ultimately, that lies at the heart of the St Clement's story. Community is what gives the London CLT its greatest potential for having lasting success, whilst at the same helping the CLT to stay rooted to its original purpose and promise. In the UK — where the provision of affordable housing has long been established through state-run council housing — it is the CLT's *relational* rather than *bureaucratic* culture, its focus on people as individuals rather than as numbers, that sets it apart.

One of the clearest examples of this relational aspect in the St Clement's process came when one of our first residents (a family who had been with the campaign throughout and had passed through the CLT's allocations process and affordability assessment) was refused a mortgage at the last minute by their lender. This was due to a technicality, based on previous debts which were not wholly theirs. In such circumstances, the easiest thing

Fig. 2.5. London CLT Annual General Meeting, 10-year anniversary, September 2017.

to do from a risk management perspective, and what most other traditional affordable housing providers would have done, would have been to rescind the offer and to go to the next family on the waiting list. But the governing board of the London CLT took a conscious decision not to do this. Instead, the board spent a lot of time and political capital negotiating with the local housing authority so as to achieve a planning amendment, which allowed the family to rent the property until they could qualify for a mortgage. That way, they could move into their new home and wouldn't have their hopes dashed yet again. The London CLT stands by our people — our mission starts and ends with them rather than rigidly following any bureaucratic or abstract quasi-utilitarian definition of "housing need."

But this family's story also illustrates a further obstacle that the London CLT has had to overcome. One of the hallmarks of doing housing development in the UK (and in much of Europe as well) is that it takes a very long time to plan, design, finance, and complete every project. This poses an enormous challenge for CLT practitioners: How do you keep prospective homebuyers interested? How do you keep the larger community of members and allies actively engaged throughout? How do you keep your power from bleeding away while waiting for something to get built?

In this regard, we would contend that building the organisation is as important as building the homes themselves. London CLT has always put a strong emphasis on its non-housing activities as a way of ensuring that our wider social justice mission is supported and sustained. One of the best examples of this — when trying in the early days to get the local community involved with the redesign of St Clements — was the work of then board members Kate MacTiernan and Lizzy Daish who, in collaboration with film director and East End resident, Danny Boyle, put on the Shuffle Film Festival for the CLT. Held over the course of a week, it opened up the St Clements site to the local community and helped them to re-engage with it, to reimagine what had been a rather sad place, and to reconceive of it as a new, accessible and exciting opportunity.

THE END OF THE BEGINNING

The London CLT at St Clements has never been just about delivering permanently affordable homes. More than that, it is about community, social justice and, quite simply, contributing to happiness in life and emotional well-being.

When our very first residents, Humayra and Ruman and their young baby Yunus, whose parents had immigrated to the East End from Bangladesh in late 1960s, moved into their new CLT home, you could see how much it meant to their whole family. In Ruman's own words:

> Before we moved into St Clement's, we were living with my parents, brother, and sister. There were six of us all in one flat. My wife (Humayra) and I shared a room whilst we had a baby on the way. It was not easy to live as a family within a family — it meant my wife felt like a stranger in her own home. I remember the day we moved in well — my whole extended family turned up. It was pouring with rain but I was beaming inside. There is so much space! I feel really lucky we get to own our own home — it has changed my family's life. There was a moment the other day when Humayra, Yunus and I were in the flat, and my Dad came over. He sat on the sofa with his arms spread out and he burst out into singing some sort of oldy goldy traditional Bengali song. My Dad only sings when he is feeling the happiest he's felt in years. That's how you know when Dad's happy; he doesn't smile, he sings. When you have that sense of space, it opens up your mind. He felt that, and he had to let it out.

Since then, Humayra has given birth to a little girl, making her the first baby born in a London CLT home! There will, we hope, be many more to come. Because the CLT movement, above all else, starts and ends with people and their lives — not housing, or resale formulas, or anything else.

To that end, many more people should be mentioned and thanked. And whilst to write an exhaustive list is impossible, and the injustice of omission is great, it would be wrong not to mention at least the incredible work along the way of Pablo Absalud, Sister Una McCreish, Fr. Sean Connolly, Fr. Tom O'Brien, David Rodgers, Peter Ambrose, Suzanne

Gormann, Miranda Housden, Professor Tim Oliver, Fr. Angus Ritchie, Bethan Lant, Ruhana Ali, Nick Durie, Colin Ivermee, Tim Carey, Joe Ball, Jenny Lumley, Neil Hunt, Lina Jamoul, Emmanuel Gatora, Sebastien Chapleau, Alison Gelder, Ruby Mahera, Nano McCaughan, Hannah Emery-Wright, Ben Cole, Grace Boyle, Charles Campion, the Butler Family Fund, and the Oak Foundation. This is as much their story as it is the story of our residents and of the homes we have built.

Whilst the first 23 homes at St Clements may not be everything we set out to achieve, and whilst they most definitely have not solved the housing crisis in our city, they have proved one thing beyond doubt: when local communities get together and organize, and when the universal principles of the CLT are carefully applied, it does not matter what city you are in, or how challenging the market may be, because what we do works. There is no mission impossible.

Fig. 2.6. Future residents of St Clements, looking out the window of their home-to-be, January 2018.

⌣

2021 POSTSCRIPT:
CREATING A CITY-WIDE, MULTI-SITE LONDON CLT

Calum Green

The first stage of London CLT's journey was about tenacity and perseverance to get London's first CLT up and running and its first homes over the line. The second stage is about our members' ambition to organise people across London to acquire land and become a city-wide, multi-site CLT.

The common thread that runs throughout both of these stages is that organised people and a clear understanding of power are how we get things done.

As Dave Smith concluded his preceding story of the early days of the London CLT, residents were just moving into their new homes at St Clements — the first project undertaken by the CLT.

Our experience in being part of acquiring and redeveloping St Clements helped us understand how hard it is to get affordable homes built in one of the world's most expensive cities. At the same time, our members were painfully aware of the continued and desperate need for truly affordable homes. They also saw neighbourhoods continuing to change without the involvement of those who already live there. So, while some London CLT members were working hard to complete St Clements, others started organising across the city to deliver the next stage of our plan.

Between 2017-2021, London CLT's membership grew from 1,000 members to over 3,400. Members signed up their friends and neighbours, and formed "community steering groups" to drive projects forward in six neighbourhoods across the city. In each of these groups, members are supported by London CLT staff to gain confidence, negotiate with people in power, build relationships with neighbours, and drive the project forward. They are given the opportunity to lead.

The focus on developing our members' capacity to lead emerged from London CLT's history of having been born out of the community organising work of Citizens UK, with whom we continue to partner. Brixton resident, and the recently elected Vice-Chair of London CLT, Razia Khanom, is the embodiment of this idea. She articulated it best:

> One evening we had a knock at the door, my husband answered. I heard people mention affordable housing, and my husband said, 'You should speak to my wife about this!'. Curious to see what was happening, I went along to the first steering group meeting. Attending the meetings again and again, I learnt about what CLTs are.
> Stepping out into the CLT group inadvertently became a journey of my own self-rediscovery. It has encouraged me to go out and get active again. It's given me a safe environment to speak to strangers. The group has also given me the courage to go back to work. Last month, after ten years out of the work environment, I secured a job! . . .

If we can do for others what LCLT has done for me, we will be well on the road to saving our communities. More leaders, more campaigns and more genuinely affordable homes.

While organising locally, our members have also worked regionally alongside partners such as Citizens UK and the National CLT Network to shift the policy environment toward creating an infrastructure supportive of CLT homes. Through this work, there is now a commitment from the Mayor of London, Sadiq Khan, to support the delivery of 1,000 CLT homes in the city. Nine local councils across London have now included community-led housing in their plans, in many cases naming CLTs explicitly. Through this commitment, local and regional opportunities for land and funding have arisen, made possible only by targeting those in power with carefully considered demands and large numbers of organised people to back them up. London CLT is well placed to enjoy these fruits of our collective political labour.

There have been some inevitable challenges that have come hand-in-hand with our ambition to grow city-wide. It has taken longer than expected for various pieces of the political infrastructure we have put in place to work together — to get funders, landowners, and CLTs to understand how best to combine forces to deliver the homes we need. London CLT has got through the most difficult parts of that challenge, but it took a lot of time to get here. And, there are many other CLTs across the UK who are still navigating the more challenging parts of that journey.

Fig. 2.7. Razia Khanon, addressing Annual General Meeting of the London CLT, 2020.

As the London CLT expands its area of work, operating in multiple neighourhoods across London, questions are raised about who and how we make decisions. We need to strike the right balance between the London-wide board's legal responsibility for the organisation and the responsibility for key development decisions that are held at the local steering group level for each community-led project. The CLT's democratic structure partly answers this challenge, but developing a culture of trust, devolving decisions to local groups of members, and maintaining lasting relationships across all levels of the organisation are important to building a truly democratic organisation.

By the middle of 2019, all of the homes at St Clements were occupied. We even had our first resale since in 2020, using our resale formula that ensured the home remained genuinely affordable to the next residents. In 2021, our second site — the first to be directly developed by us — Brasted Close in Lewisham, south London — has started construction on 11 permanently affordable homes. We also have agreements on land for a further six sites for around 140 homes, and are in discussions with landowners on three additional sites.

London has a £38m Community Housing Fund that London CLT is well placed to take advantage of, and a commitment from the Mayor for 1,000 community-led homes. We can now truly say we are a city-wide, multi-site CLT.

What next for London CLT? First, we need to deliver. Our members, and the wider CLT movement, have pushed many powers-that-be to support CLTs. Now we need to deliver the permanently affordable, high-quality, and well-managed homes we said we could. The prize is big — thousands of Londoners across our city acting in solidarity to deliver the homes their neighbourhoods need. This is no small task, and will require a laser-like focus on our own operational performance.

After that? Well, as a democratic organisation, that is up to our members. They will set our future direction.

3.

Messy Is Good!
Origins and Evolution of the
CLT Movement in England

Stephen Hill, Catherine Harrington, and Tom Archer

"Housing is a messy subject." This was the insight of Professor Sir Michael Atiyah, former president of the Royal Society and arguably the United Kingdom's greatest mathematician since Isaac Newton. He made this remark in his opening speech to an international symposium of scientists in 1998, convened to propose "A Global Strategy for Housing in the Third Millennium." Hosted by the Royal Society, the symposium was intended to have a strong scientific and technological bias, but Sir Atiyah focused on morality and human rights:

> Housing is not scientific, not hard. Its themes are living, love, family, sociability and self-expression; none of which is easily quantified or measured . . . Sunshine may be more important than solar energy, and community and comfort are more important than strength and durability . . .

Another speaker, John P. Eberhard, Professor of Architecture and Planning at Carnegie Mellon University, moved swiftly from design codes and concrete testing procedures to call for a new paradigm of housing research, based on housing rights. He was scornful of "the continuing power of preferred positions" and the negligible contributions made by governments and construction industries to housing the homeless and people on modest incomes in both the developed and developing world:

> The housing industry in Western society prefers the status quo, and will not support government research programmes that might upset the "delicate balance" of the housing markets . . . I present here a case for making changes in the national housing priorities of Western societies, and argue that housing issues are interwoven with the issues of community infrastructure. . . . The barriers to effective technological solutions or design changes in housing are primarily questions of political will . . .

Barriers, industry preferring the status quo, political will (or the absence of it)—those will sound like familiar challenges to anyone working to meet the housing needs of their own community. That includes community land trusts, since producing and preserving affordable housing has been the main focus of England's CLT movement. This chapter will focus on how CLT activists in England have met the messy challenges of housing and steadily rebuilt the infrastructure in their communities, despite everything that seemed to get in the way.

This is also a story of how CLTs have reshaped political will and national policy in a country where policymaking for both housing and community development has been highly centralized; as if there were one English housing market, rather than hundreds of smaller markets. CLTs and their allies among other forms of community-led housing have helped to redesign and to redirect national policy so that local priorities, autonomy, and diversity are valued and supported—objectives that have now been substantially achieved.

The chapter covers three periods, mapping the trajectory of CLT development in England:

- Period One, 1986–2008: "Origins of CLT Thinking and Practice."

- Period Two, 2008–2018: "A Decade of Growth and Consolidation."

- Period Three, Present and Beyond: "Potential Futures for CLTs."

This chapter will celebrate the importance of "messiness" in the development of new ways of doing things in a field of activity that has historically been resistant to change and dominated by many vested political and financial interests. English CLTs are concerned both with the specific provision of genuinely and permanently affordable housing, and with what some CLTs have called "local governance," the power of self-determination on issues that are of critical importance to the wellbeing of a community.[1] Over three decades, messiness has helped to build a resilient and adaptive CLT movement, one that is now capable of generating enough possible and appropriate futures to keep that movement in good shape.

I. ORIGINS OF CLT THINKING AND PRACTICE, 1986–2008

- *Reimagining the equity structure of housing and land in villages, towns and cities.* The need for new locally based institutions to promote financial inclusion and to hold land for the common good emerged during an extended period of political change, created by financial crises and the distortion of local housing markets by the deregulation of global capital.

▪ *Improving the quality of life in rural Cornwall.* New ways of providing permanently affordable housing through CLTs arose in places where no other organisation could or would provide it.

▪ *New institutions for devolved local governance* emerged in government programmes, public housing estate regeneration, land assembly in the public interest, and urban renewal and growth area settings.

▪ *A statutory definition for CLTs in England and Wales* was enacted, emphasizing the "community" in CLT.

Reimagining the Equity Structure of Housing and Land in Villages, Towns and Cities[2]

The 1980s were a period of significant change in patterns of property ownership, financial services, and corporate ownership. Post-war welfare state policies were under assault on two fronts: from the privatisation of publicly funded and publicly owned assets and services, and from the deregulation of global capital markets. Before 1985, the biggest mortgage providers were mutual building societies. Trustee Savings Banks (TSB), with links to local government, provided low-cost banking services for working-class populations. Utilities were all publicly owned. Land ownership by central and local government had grown since the 1920s with the development of public housing, the building of post-WWII New Towns, and with a wide range of amenities for the "common good," including community and youth centres, swimming pools, and parks.

All this was to change. De-mutualisation led to the widespread transfer of almost all the large building societies and TSB networks to the United Kingdom's "Big Five" banks. Utilities, local buses, and train services were sold to private companies. The Conservative government's Right to Buy policy in 1980 led to the sale of council homes at generous discounts. By 2019, there were 1.25 million fewer affordable homes of all kinds than in 1980, despite all the new building that had occurred.

As banks closed branches, inner-city and rural communities were increasingly denied access to even the most basic financial services, marking a growing trend of financial exclusion for people on low and moderate incomes. Recession in the early 1990s made things worse, ushering in a time of persistently high levels of unemployment in those same inner-city and rural areas. The crisis accelerated the decline of manufacturing employment in northern England, with firms going into liquidation or relocating abroad in search of cheaper labour and more lenient regulation.

Local governments lost resources, powers, and autonomy. The central government restricted their ability to borrow and, thus, their capacity to build their own affordable housing or to assist private homeowners and landlords in improving the aging stock of terraced homes built in the 19th Century, which still formed the main source of housing in inner-city areas. With the sale of public-sector housing stock, a sharp fall across the UK in new house building, and a tidal wave of deregulated mortgage finance flooding the market, house prices rose much faster than incomes, marking the start of the process of financialisation of land and property markets. That process continues to this day, especially in London, Oxford, Cambridge and much of southern England. In many rural areas, the growth of second or holiday homeownership, and the retirement to the country of older people with accumulated housing equity from the sale of valuable urban homes, added to the upward drift in house prices.

The first pioneering CLT, the Stonesfield Trust, was set up in rural Oxfordshire in the mid-1980s. Like many other villages, rising housing prices had made Oxfordshire unaffordable for local people on a low or moderate income, but no one was building new, affordably priced homes. The Trust's founder, Tony Crofts, lived in the village and donated a small site to the Trust, an organization he had helped to set up. It was controlled by people living in the village, and aimed to provide permanently affordable rental housing for people who needed to live and work locally. The development was completed at relatively low cost, using a creative mix of investment by Crofts, loans from the local council and two social banks (Ecology Building Society and Triodos Bank) and interest-free loans and donations from the Quaker Housing Trust and ethical investors. In 1994, the equity of the first homes was used as leverage to build three more CLT homes and two affordable workspaces. This alignment of mutual interests among the community, a local landowner, the council, and funders was to be the foundation for the many rural CLTs that followed.

> They were all searching for alternative institutions that could tackle social and economic exclusion.

Crofts was a Quaker, who had been inspired by the writings of Gerard Winstanley and the Diggers, and by their ambition that land should be a "common store-house for all." Although he initiated his CLT project independently, he soon made connections with a group of activists working on new ways of addressing the impact of these wider structural changes. They were all searching for alternative institutions that could tackle social and economic exclusion, especially those that could encourage democratic and community ownership of housing, such as community land trusts.

This group of activists was greatly influenced by a 1989 book edited by Ward Morehouse, *Building Sustainable Communities*.[3] It included chapters by Shann Turnbull from Australia and Bob Swann and George Benello from the USA, highlighting the links among Community Development Finance Institutions (CDFIs), CLTs, and worker co-ops.[4]

In the late 1990s, several activists travelled to the USA from England, where they met Bob Swann, co-founder of the Institute of Community Economics, and John Davis who had helped to start the Burlington CLT (now named the Champlain Housing Trust). Their visit to the USA left them convinced that the development of CDFIs and CLTs, as new sustainable institutions to combat financial and social exclusion, would require the establishment of a nationally available support service and a treasury of retained knowledge that would make CLTs replicable and possible for any urban or rural community.

In 1999, after creating a formal action group, they developed terms of reference for a CLT action research programme and helped to establish Community Finance Solutions (CFS) at the University of Salford. CFS took the lead on policy advocacy for the growth of new CDFIs and CLTs, backed by other activists, who provided practical support for new CLT projects until the National CLT Network was formed in 2010.

The action research brief aimed to test how a CDFI and CLT strategy for rural regeneration could be aligned to win support from communities, local government, and funders. The first project was funded by the Hastoe Housing Association (a specialist rural affordable housing association), and the Housing Corporation (the government agency responsible for promoting and funding affordable housing in England). Three rural areas of England were selected for the action research. The project looked at the combined effects of the growth in second homes and a series of farming crises which had devastated rural economies across England throughout the 1990s. The most hard-hit of these areas was the southwest of England — Cornwall in particular.

Improving the Quality of Life in Rural Cornwall through Community Land Trusts[5]

That Cornwall became the first, and remains one of the most progressive and successful areas for CLTs, was the result of an ideal alignment of special circumstances that would shape the future development of CLTs. It was also due in part to the work of Dr. Bob Paterson (who lived just over the Cornish border in Devon) and by others at Community Finance Solutions.[6] Between 1999 and 2006, Community Finance Solutions began to develop practical ways of securing community ownership of land as the best way of providing permanently affordable housing.

After several years of planning, the Cornwall Community Land Trust (CCLT) began work in 2006, forming into a company in 2007. It aimed to advance CLTs by providing practical advice and support to village communities wishing to establish their own CLTs. Having an experienced housing development manager (Alan Fox) in the role of CCLT's Project Director, was instrumental.

Vital seed-corn funding was sourced from local councils and the forward-thinking Tudor Trust. A critically important relationship was forged with the project host, Cornwall Rural Housing Association (CRHA), whose chief executive at the time had previous experience in the cooperative business sector. This relationship saw back-office support and selective project finance provided by CRHA, with the Cornwall CLT providing development management services to CRHA. This cross-fertilisation of activity underpinned the financial viability of the CCLT. The success of this model of locally provided technical support was to lead, eventually, to the development of similar "Umbrella CLTs" across the country at the county, city, and sub-regional levels.

"I've lived in a caravan for all of this year, and was just really worried about what I was going to do and where I was going to live. Now, having my own home and building it myself with a garden in a place like this—it's just unreal."—new homeowner, St. Minver CLT

St. Minver, a pioneering self-build CLT. The parish of St. Minver includes a number of holiday villages on the north Cornwall coast, with some of the best surfing beaches in the UK. In 2006, average house prices were higher than in London. This caused proactive local parish councillors to begin exploring ways to overcome the difficulty experienced by local people in finding affordable housing to rent or to buy.

The St. Minver Community Land Trust Ltd emerged when a parish councillor sowed the idea of forming a CLT, when a local farmer offered land at a low price, and when a local builder and a group of residents came together. The North Cornwall District Council provided a start-up grant and an interest-free loan to underpin the development of what turned out to be the first of three phases. The self-build mortgages enabled the purchase of a serviced self-build plot from the CLT and repayment of the Council's loan. The St. Minver CLT was supported and advised by CCLT. A local allocation/sales policy was agreed with the Council, and twelve self-build applicants were selected from local people in need.

The St. Minver CLT signed a Section 106 Agreement with the local Council: a legally binding planning obligation which controls future occupancy and affordability and must be adhered to by all successive owner-occupants of a CLT home. The Section 106 Agreement is an additional protection for the principle of affordability in perpetuity. The same principle is embodied in the CLT's constitution and is incorporated into the sale of homes to income-qualified buyers.

The CLT completed its first phase of homes in Dingle's Way in December 2008, on time and on budget. They were sold on limited-equity terms. The total cost of the home represented one-third of the market value of the home on the day of completion, deemed to be affordable to local people paying no more than one-third of Area Median Income to meet their housing costs. This transformed the lives of local families who, without the CLT, would never have found secure housing. All future resales will be priced at one-third the market value of the home, with a new qualifying buyer selected by the CLT.

A partnership between the St. Minver CLT and CRHA has since seen a second phase of eight more self-build, limited-equity homes and four other rented homes completed on adjoining land in 2011. The CLT is now planning a third development in another part of the Parish.

What was the key to success for the Cornwall CLT? Three critical factors enabled Cornwall to become a rural CLT hotspot:

- Credible and sustained community leadership at the village and council level;

- Local councils offering short-term development finance through Revolving Loan Funds; and

- An alignment of interests among the council, local landowners, the CLT, and a local housing association, ensuring community support and leadership to identify appropriate sites, matched with access to locally available technical expertise.[7]

What was the key lesson from Cornwall that informed the future growth of CLTs nationwide? Individuals and organizations that had backed CLT development in Cornwall hoped to see the model spread throughout the UK. That would require, in their estimation, two building blocks. First, some sort of "national demonstration programme" was needed to refine the CLT concept, to influence public policy, and to widen acceptance of the CLT model by communities in other rural areas. Second, equity was needed to support initial experimentation and early replication of the CLT model, providing risk capital that would enable new CLTs to take on repayable debt for their first projects and to establish a track record of effective performance. Both building blocks were put in place by 2008. (The purpose and importance of the National CLT Demonstration Programme and the CLT Fund are described below, under Period II.)

New Institutions for Devolved Local Governance in Government Regeneration and Growth Area Programmes

The third strand of the early CLT story is fundamentally different. In rural areas, it had been community leaders, activists, and residents who had taken the initiative to find a solution to local problems which neither the state nor anyone else was trying to solve. In the national policy arena, the initiative for finding new ways to involve communities in housing provision and urban regeneration, thereby winning a place for CLTs, fell to a group of activist professionals: housing and public administration lawyers and specialists in housing development and finance. Their professional work was motivated by a public interest commitment to ensuring that citizens and communities woud have an effective say in major decisions that affect their lives.

These activist professionals were to play a major role in promoting and positioning CLTs to become a potential instrument of housing policy, particularly as related to:

- Methods of land assembly in government-designated Growth Areas;

- New forms of local governance to promote community wellbeing, through effective stewardship programmes for community-owned or community-controlled land; and

- The regeneration of large urban public housing estates.[8]

Although results on the ground were limited at the time, the presence of CLTs in pub-lic policy thinking were nevertheless critical to the development of the concept.

Methods of land assembly in Growth Areas.[9] The Labour Party, which led Britain's gov-ernment from 1997 to 2010, backed a major expansion in housing supply, starting with its 2003 Sustainable Communities Plan, reinforced by major planning law reforms enact-ed in 2004. These measures aimed to empower citizens in local development of all kinds, requiring every development to have a Statement of Community Involvement.[10]

Organisations like the Joseph Rowntree Foundation believed that community own-ership of land for new housing development could be a powerful way to engage com-munities in the future of their places, while reducing opposition to new development. That was based on its own experience with community control of development and local governance at its New Earswick development.[11] In its 2002 Centenary Year Report *Land for Housing,* the Foundation included a technical appendix explaining how CLTs could be used to secure a long-term community interest in land for new development.[12]

CLTs were also advocated by the Local Government Association (LGA) in its 2004 publication, *New Development and New Opportunities.* Although councils had very few powers, resources, or political inclination to take advantage of these "new opportunities," LGA's endorsement helped to raise the profile of CLTs and to popularize the concept.

> "A community land trust is a private non-profit corporation created
> to acquire and hold land for the benefit of a community and provide
> secure affordable access to land and housing for community residents.
> In particular, community land trusts attempt to meet the needs of
> residents least served by the prevailing market."
>
> —Local Government Association (2004)

New forms of local governance to promote community wellbeing, through the stewardship of community-owned or community-controlled assets. Alongside its planning reforms, the Labour government wanted to "modernise" local government. The New Deal for Com-munities (NDC), developed by the Labour government of the time, was a refinement of earlier urban regeneration programmes that had focussed on housing. It invested about £5 million annually in each of twenty deprived neighbourhoods (each containing up to 15,000 people) over a period of ten years. In 1998, councils and communities bid jointly for funding. Once selected, communities were put "in charge" of these resources. How-ever, the central government failed to make councils cooperate with the NDC commu-nities, thus seriously weakening the impact of this programme. Even so, a few successful NDC bodies continued after public funding ended in 2009.[13]

The NDC programme formed part of a more systemic approach to local government, integrating the use of assets, finance, town planning, and public service delivery. This approach was embedded in the Local Government Act of 2000, in which councils were given express powers to do anything they wished to promote the social, economic, and environmental wellbeing of their communities, a purpose that would later be reflected in the statutory definition of CLTs.

The regeneration of large urban public housing estates. From the late 1980s through the early 2000s, both Conservative and Labour governments funded capital programmes that enabled councils to improve aging or structurally defective public housing estates. Funding conditions often required councils to include communities in both decision making about the projects and the long-term governance of estates. Until the Financial Crash in 2007, the government's Community Housing Taskforce was investigating the potential for community-controlled CLTs to own the freehold of their estates, leasing the land to housing associations who would upgrade or redevelop this social housing.

A Statutory Definition for CLTs in England and Wales: Why There's a "C" in CLT

The activist professionals who were operating in this political environment had been inspired by the success of the Dudley Street Neighborhood Initiative (DSNI) in Boston.[14] DSNI's governance and holistic regeneration achievements were regarded as potential exemplars for both councils and communities that were being affected by plans for regeneration and new housing development.

The kind of devolved autonomy from the state, which DSNI respresented, was promoted by activist professionals in England as a model of "double devolution." This policy, adopted by the Labour government in the early 2000s, was intended to achieve a progressive devolution of powers from central to local government and from local government to communities. The Minister of Local Government considered various ideas for implementing devolution through his Local Government Sounding Board.[15] The Local Government Association, however, had no interest in the idea of transferring any powers to communities, despite its earlier endorsement of CLTs in the context of new development.

What the activists learned from this experience — and from the frustration of various CLT initiatives not quite coming off — was that CLT development could not be sustained in the face of shifting market or political conditions, unless "community" was the driving force behind the process. Even well-intentioned politicians, public servants, and professionals were no substitute for community leadership, advocacy, and organising in making CLTs happen.

Nevertheless, the activists appreciated the necessity for CLTs to obtain sufficient legal recognition that would justify a corporate existence independent of any particular government policy or programme, and any transitory political party alignment. In Corn-wall, where CLTs were starting their first homes in 2007, it was especially apparent that having a national legal definition for CLTs would open up more sources of finance. Lend-ers were beginning to be more cautious as the Financial Crash unfolded. They needed a standardized definition of the CLT to understand what kind of organisation they were being asked to support in financing new residential development.

This Cornish justification for enacting a CLT definition was a straightforward "ask" of Members of Parliament (MPs). An amendment was added to the Housing and Regenera-tion Bill that was going through Parliament, specifying how a "community land trust" was to be defined in England and Wales. It was enacted into law in 2008.

Definition of a Community Land Trust in England and Wales: Section 79, Housing and Regeneration Act 2008

A corporate body which satisfies the conditions below:

1. is established for the express purpose of furthering the social, economic and environmental interests of a local community by acquiring and managing land and other assets in order:
  - to provide a benefit to the local community; and
  - to ensure that the assets are not sold or developed except in a manner which the trust's members think benefits the local community

2. is established under arrangements which are expressly designed to ensure that:
  - any profits from its activities will be used to benefit the local community (otherwise than by being paid directly to members); and
  - individuals who live or work in the specified area have the opportunity to become members of the trust (whether or not others can also become members) and the members of a trust control it.

The wording of this statutory definition was not just intended to reassure lending institutions, however. It was even more relevant for communities needing a legal form through which they could become more powerful in decision making about the future of their areas. By linking a CLT's purpose to the ownership of land for promoting the inter-ests of residents, the definition tried to remedy the democratic deficit that had been left by the government's abandonment of "double devolution." It also addressed the absence of any obligation of landowners to serve the "common good" in English property rights and law.

Embodied in this CLT definition were three essential (and quietly subversive) con-cepts that would empower communities in the planning, development, and regeneration of their local areas:

▪ A CLT could only exist to protect and promote the economic, social and environmental interests of the existing community (directly copying the wellbeing powers given to councils in the Local Government Act 2000, and the legal purposes attributed to the planning reforms in the Planning and Compulsory Purchase Act 2004);

▪ Land should be owned and used for purposes of securing the "common good"; and

▪ Participatory, democratic control and democratic influence should be hallmarks of local development.

For most community activists, their main motivation for setting up a CLT was to restrict the price of land, curbing an out-of-control land market that was working against the wellbeing of their communities. This represented an approach to the pricing and allocation of land that elected and appointed public officials were (and still are) reluctant to adopt. The definition's overriding purpose was, therefore, to give communities status and democratic legitimacy to act in their own interests, pursuing a strategy that did not have to be decided by either the central or local government.

II. GROWTH AND CONSOLIDATION, 2008–2018

If the previous two decades sowed the seeds for a CLT movement in England, the third decade saw its rapid germination, as CLTs grew from twenty at the start of 2008 to over 300 today.[16] Crucially, this occurred during a period of further political and economic upheaval.

In 2010, after the first General Election following the 2007 Financial Crash, the new Coalition Government embarked on a radical reshaping of housing policy. This was aimed at bolstering private housebuilding and renting, whilst squeezing out affordable housing provision. Despite aspirations to tackle the "housing crisis," the government was spending 44% less public money on affordable homes by 2013, with knock-on secondary effects that limited CLT growth in some ways and stimulated it in others.

Council budgets, hit hard by austerity policies, severely limited the ability of councils to invest in housing and regeneration. In this new world of market-driven housing production and state retrenchment, civil society organisations like CLTs were expected to flourish as part of the Coalition Government's new idea: the "Big Society."

Despite being personally championed by the Prime Minister, David Cameron, the Big Society soon lost political traction. A few of his ideas survived into the Localism Act 2011, however, which introduced new community rights for civil society organisations. Neighbourhood Planning, the right to draw up a hyper-local plan, has been the most significant and widely used of these. The qualifying criteria for community organisations using this right were closely modelled on the CLT statutory definition, enacted three years earlier.

Fig. 3.1. CLT housing under construction in Dorset, England. Despite astronomical land values, unstable ground, the withdrawal of government grants, and unfavourable planning policy, the Lyme Regis CLT persisted. Nothing could stop them!

Yet the development of CLTs continued to be held back by familiar challenges: access to land, funding, and finance; local planning processes; deficits in technical knowledge and skills; and limited public acceptance of affordable housing in certain areas. With so many barriers standing in the way of CLTs, the eventual emergence of today's CLT movement is remarkable. How did this happen? What made it possible? What were the pivotal moments in its development?

We shall answer these questions by describing this stage of growth of the CLT movement through four parallel strands of activity:

- Building a support infrastructure;

- Making the voice of CLTs heard in government;

- Speaking in a united voice to government, advocating for all forms of community-led housing; and

- Improving the funding and finance system.

Building a Support Infrastructure

Despite public enthusiasm for CLTs, very few groups had actually built any homes before 2008. This was due, in part, to there being no support infrastructure to capitalise on this interest. A persuasive argument that such an infrastructure was needed was put forward by activists, academics, and professionals who had been making the case for CLTs. They convinced the Carnegie UK Trust, the Housing Corporation, and the Higher Education Funding Council for England to support an initial two-year National CLT Demonstration Programme, starting in 2008. Led by Community Finance Solutions, the goals of this programme were to promote the creation of CLTs — in both rural and urban settings — and to provide advice and support to local groups so they could get their projects off the ground.[17]

On a parallel track, the same activists successfully assembled the capital for a "CLT Fund" from a number of major charitable foundations. This Fund provided small seed-corn grants to cover the start-up stages of CLTs and offered pre-development and development loans for CLT projects.[18]

By the end of the Demonstration Programme, three CLTs were in the process of building 30 homes and another 139 homes were in the pipeline.[19] New resources and technical advice also emerged. But enabling support remained limited, political support was marginal, and the CLT movement still lacked a united voice.

Following the Demonstration Programme's final recommendations, a Community Empowerment Grant was secured from the central government in 2010, providing initial funding for two essential elements of a support infrastructure for CLTs:

- A national membership body; and

- A replicable sub-regional enabling body, called an "Umbrella CLT," using Wessex Community Assets as the pilot.

The National CLT Network was started in 2010, with a blank slate in terms of its future form and direction. The first director, who was the organisation's sole paid employee at the time, was assigned a dizzying array of initial tasks: establish governance and membership arrangements; provide support and resources for emerging groups; communicate with communities and the national and local press; and lobby central government to address barriers to CLT development. It was also vital to ensure that the first CLT members took ownership of the national mission and participated in the new organisation's governance. The Network would have credibility only if it was a genuinely representative body.

The choice of an appropriate host for the Network was important. After considering a number of civil society organisations with housing and community interests, the National Housing Federation, the representative body for housing associations in England, was selected. The Federation offered the greatest potential to increase the coverage and influence of the Network's activity, despite representing a somewhat different set of housing interests from those of the Network.

The interests of the Federation and the Network did indeed diverge between 2010 and 2014, as many housing associations became larger, more corporate, and less connected to the communities they served. Also, with the growing profile and standing of the Network, there was sufficient impetus to become legally and operationally independent; which it did in June 2014.

Umbrella CLTs —Building the Sub-regional Support Infrastructure. The Network quickly learnt that, despite the growing number of CLTs forming since 2010, the scale and pace of development would be limited if CLTs continued to rely solely on volunteers. These individuals were being asked to learn vast amounts of technical information about housing finance, company law, and development planning; in essence, becoming quasi-housing professionals, while supported by a small number of sympathetic and committed advisers willing to travel the country. Seed-corn funding from the CLT Fund, which paid for early advisory support, only took these fledgling CLTs a short way on their journey. Many could only move slowly toward reaching their goal of building homes.

Stronger support systems were required. One such system was emerging in the form of "Umbrella CLTs," including those in Cornwall, Cumbria, Lincolnshire, the East of England, and Somerset, Devon, and Dorset (Wessex). In theory, umbrella CLTs could offer end-to-end support for both organizational and project development. Each covered an entire county or several counties, supporting individual CLTs in that area, from the initial start-up stage of a CLT being a "bright idea," through incorporation, planning, and construction, to the point where people moved into new CLT homes. Some Umbrella CLTs like Wessex were based on strong partnerships with carefully chosen housing associations having shared aims and values. This enabled communities to focus on being effective participants in shaping projects, with the housing association taking on the technical and administrative burden, bringing its expertise in development and financing.

The Network actively sought funding from charitable foundations and government to support the establishment of new Umbrellas, hoping to achieve full geographic coverage of England. As these regional and sub-regional support systems grew, the Network saw that its role needed to change; it should only do what could not be adequately performed at the local, sub-regional, or regional level. This meant focusing on national advocacy campaigns, leadership, and promotion of best practices.

Making the Voice of CLTs Heard in Government— Experiments and Successes in Advocacy

Despite having secured a statutory definition for CLTs in 2008, political support for CLTs was still tentative. It became a priority of the Network to strengthen the influence of CLTs with central government and to secure capital grant funding for the development of CLT projects.

The value of CLTs could only be demonstrated when politicians could see a sufficient number of completed CLT homes. But land acquisition and housing development required some form of capitalization by government. In England, social housing was supported through the central government's Affordable Homes Programme for housing associations. In response to lobbying, £25m of that Programme was set aside for CLTs up to 2015. This supported a number of projects, particularly in areas like Wessex, where the housing association partnership model and Umbrella CLT support meant that a good number of rural schemes could progress relatively quickly.

Using public money in this way did not meet with universal support, however. Some academics and community activists saw CLTs as a critique of past housing policy failures and current forms of publicly supported housing. They argued that CLTs should draw on entirely different sources of finance and be independent of central government and its ideas about tenure and affordability. The Network had to navigate a fine line between demonstrating that CLTs were a practicable, preferable choice, therefore, creating valuable social and economic outcomes, whilst simultaneously holding onto the principle that CLTs must only develop what is locally appropriate and desired, not what is decided at a government official's desk in central London.

The 2015 General Election provided a key opportunity for the Network to mobilise its lobbying experience to influence the major parties, and any new government's policies. The Network's pre- and post-election manifestos made ambitious demands, including capital grants and funding for support and advice, and for preferential treatment of CLT projects in planning, taxation, and leasehold law.

The Network moved beyond its traditional lobbying and influencing at the national level, which had focused on government ministers, MPs, political advisors and think-tanks. It focused simultaneously on the grassroots, mobilising individual CLTs to lobby their MPs, particularly in electorally significant areas, knowing that the constituency link would prove critical in gaining MPs' support, thereby influencing national policymaking.

New urban CLTs were also showing how targeted lobbying and community organising could secure political commitments at the local and regional level. Community organisers at Citizens UK and at the London CLT extracted commitments to support CLTs from public officials. This culminated in support from London's mayors (first Ken Livingstone, and then Boris Johnson) for the first significant urban CLT project in the UK, located at the St Clements Hospital site in London's East End.

Over 80 MPs were targeted in the run-up to the General Election, many of whom pledged their support for the Network's pre-election manifesto. Once the new Government was elected, the Network, knowing that there could not be a political "ask" without a matching political "offer," set out a convincing case to government officials that CLTs could help them to achieve their own housing aspirations by:

- Gaining popular support for new housebuilding, which was often fiercely resisted by established communities directly affected by development;

- Helping diversify the house building industry after the Financial Crash, which had accelerated the demise of small- and medium-sized builders and developers;

- Innovating in an industry highly resistant to change; and

- Addressing affordability concerns for both middle-income and low-income households in electorally sensitive areas.

Despite the cross-party appeal of CLTs, one of the new government's first actions was to introduce a Housing and Planning Bill into Parliament that, amongst other measures, imposed a compulsory rent-reduction regime for social housing providers that would have left several CLTs bankrupt within 2–3 years. The government also proposed extending the existing Right to Buy to the tenants of housing associations. This would have provided tenants with a large discount to purchase their homes, including some CLT homes,[20] directly undermining the ability of CLTs to keep their homes genuinely affordable in perpetuity. The potential damage to the CLT brand, and thus the risk to the future of the CLT movement as a whole, was significant.

A twin-track national-local lobbying strategy proved critical in enabling the Network to move quickly to protect CLTs from the Bill's most damaging features. The lobbying presence in Whitehall, combined with pressure from CLTs on the ground, was highly effective in winning CLT exemptions to both rent reduction and Right to Buy proposals. Within Whitehall, the Network had gained a reputation for being an effective lobbying organisation, with Ministers repeatedly approached by MPs on behalf of CLTs within their constituencies.

A United Voice Promoting All Forms of Community-Led Housing

From the mid–2000s, attempts had been made to collaborate among the main national representative bodies of housing cooperatives, CLTs, cohousing communities, and development trusts: all forms of "community-led housing" (CLH).[21]

The aim of collaboration was to project a more powerful sector voice in national debates. Working together proved challenging for everyone. Each body started out believing they had more to gain by lobbying separately on behalf of their own memberships. They were torn between protecting their identity and promoting policies specific to their model, versus supporting a wider set of shared activities and objectives. CLTs, in particular, had a unique focus on lasting affordability, which was not universally shared among the other CLH sector bodies. Nevertheless, the CLT Network decided to take a more inclusive stance vis-à-vis other national bodies and to play a significant leadership role within this sector, because the Network's director and trustees judged that CLTs would benefit from being part of a larger landscape of community-led housing.

In 2015, World Habitat (formerly the Building and Social Housing Foundation) helpfully stepped in at this juncture. World Habitat, with its global experience of community-led housing, could act as an independent broker to forge alliances across the sector. This was fortunate timing. The first alliance between national bodies was forged between the National CLT Network and the UK Cohousing Network. The growing stature of the former and a gradual alignment of aims and values between the two Networks resulted in them sharing staff and back-office functions, and lobbying government together. The two Networks then led the efforts to bring on board the other CLH sector bodies to endorse a broader vision and to present a united front to central government. Those efforts eventually paid off. The four main national bodies now work collaboratively in a formal alliance called Community Led Homes.[22]

> The four national bodies now work collaboratively in a formal alliance.

Improving the System of Funding and Finance

Most early CLTs drew on a diverse range of funding and finance to make their projects viable, as the Stonesfield CLT had done. The CLT Fund had been designed to provide CLTs with both pre-development and development loans structured in innovative ways. Some were provided "at risk," repayable only if and when planning permission was granted. Other loans were available with lower levels of security, taking a subordinate position on the property to enable a larger lender to take the first position. By the end of 2018, the CLT Fund had supported over 44 CLTs and had helped to finance over 100 newly built affordable homes, with another 400+ in development.[23]

Whilst helpful, these funds were still no panacea, especially for groups trying to cover pre-development costs on larger projects. Other funds became available, such as the reallocation of £14m unspent Government revenue funding (from another Community Rights programme); however, the government's conditions were highly risk averse, requiring groups to have bought or secured a firm interest in their site before the government's money would be released.

Other forms of niche funding were developed, especially as interest grew in urban CLTs. A generous grant from the Oak Foundation enabled the Network to set up a dedicated Urban CLT Project, providing small grants and peer-to-peer learning for twenty pioneering urban CLTs over a period of three years. Some were in areas with very high land values; others were in areas with lower land values and a large number of empty homes. The programme also supported the first Welsh CLT in Rhyl. Recent evaluations of the Urban CLT Project highlight the critical role of seed-corn funding in leveraging wider investment for urban schemes, and showed how urban CLTs have the potential to amass large memberships which strengthen their political leverage at a local level.

The Network was also intent on trying to create a more coherent eco-system of funding and finance, with a wider range of loans on sensible and appropriate terms for community

Fig. 3.2. Catherine Harrington, Co-Chief Executive of the National CLT Network and Anna Kear, Executive Director of the UK Cohousing Network, join forces to welcome Minister of State for Housing, Alok Sharma MP, to their community-led housing conference in 2017, at which he announced the next stage of the Community Housing Fund.

groups. Social investors and ethical lenders, such as the Charity Bank, Triodos Bank, and the Ecology Building Society, stepped forward to offer new financial products. Much of this was highly bespoke, however, and still left significant gaps.

The Community Housing Fund. For the General Election in May 2015, the Network's manifesto had asked for renewed capital funding for CLTs, similar to the £25m Affordable Housing Programme that had just ended in March 2015. When the government's first budget was unveiled in March 2016, the Network, and indeed the whole CLH sector, were delighted to hear the Chancellor announce a £60m Community Housing Fund for community housing projects in rural and coastal areas, notably where there was a high proportion of high-priced second homes. Surprisingly, civil servants then confirmed that the fund was, in fact, £60m for each of the next five years (later reduced to four years); so £240m overall, considerably more than anything the CLH sector had seen previously.

Creation of the Community Housing Fund was a clear vindication of the Network's leadership and lobbying efforts. It provided a unique opportunity to build on the work of the preceding years, creating a stronger infrastructure and a coherent system of funding and finance for CLH groups.

The CLT and Cohousing Networks took the lead in articulating a vison and practical design for the Community Housing Fund, and led efforts to bring on board the other CLH sector bodies. The Government adopted this vision.

The Community Housing Fund is available to CLH groups across England and consists of:

- Revenue grants to set up new groups and to get them development-ready;

- Capital grants for infrastructure and the construction of affordable homes of any tenure; and

- Grants to create the national support infrastructure, building on the concept of Umbrella CLTs to create a national network of local Enabling Hubs.

General Lessons for Building and Sustaining a National CLT Movement, 2008–2018

A decade of rapid CLT growth in England and Wales offers several key lessons for movement building:

- *Lesson 1.* Lobbying efforts proved highly effective: a result of the division of tasks between the Network and communities on the ground. Individually, CLTs harnessed the power of telling their local stories to persuade those with influence and decision-making power, especially in electorally sensitive areas. The Network provided the mobilisation, information for CLTs on the key "asks" of decision makers, and the technical and policy-centred arguments in favour of CLTs. Most critically, it exerted direct influence on Ministers and significant MPs.

- *Lesson 2.* The success of the national lobbying activity flowed from a pragmatic approach, framing CLTs within the wider housing crisis and aligning CLTs with dominant ideological and political priorities. Government ministers and officials were shown how CLTs and other CLH initiatives could help them to achieve their national housing objectives.

- *Lesson 3.* Having sold the political benefits of CLTs, lobbying was directed toward influencing financial priorities, expanding access to land and finance, and enacting legal and legislative rules affecting the viability of CLT models of development.

- *Lesson 4.* The Network and local CLTs developed a clear picture of the financial requirements of CLTs over the lifetime of their projects, including: revenue for core activities, capital for land acquisition and project development, and ongoing revenue to allow CLTs to play a long-term stewardship role. CLTs need more than money. Networks of skilled professionals are required to reduce the burdens on volunteers. The argument for Enabling Hubs, which are supporting CLTs across the country, appears to have prevailed. Only time will tell, however, if that infrastucture is sustainable.

III. POTENTIAL FUTURES FOR CLTs

* Reinventing "left behind" rural towns, in the context of neighbourhood or other community-led plans to tackle housing, employment, heritage and landscape challenges in towns that get little if any support from public policy initiatives or public resources.

* Establishing "enabling hubs" and civic partnerships with city authorities, aspiring to greater devolution from the central government.

Reinventing "Left Behind" Rural Towns[24]

Cranbrook and Sissinghurst Parish lies in the glorious rolling farmland of the High Weald in Kent: a protected area of outstanding natural beauty and one of the most complete medieval landscapes in Europe. With 130 historic farmsteads, the Parish is brimming with archaeology. Architecture and place names tell of a legacy of invasion and immigration from mainland Europe.

Cranbrook town prides itself on its independent retail centre, and has more ancient buildings than many larger historic cathedral cities, many dating to the time of the medieval cloth industry, when its economy first peaked. Cranbrook also has the tallest windmill in England, a lofty medieval church, a quirky provincial museum, a theatre, and a year-round arts programme.

Even so, the town is not thriving. Outward prosperity conceals internal economic and social weaknesses. Cranbrook has lost both its rail link and its market. It does not benefit from any special programmes of government financial support. Like many other parts of the UK that voted to leave the European Union in 2016, the citizens of Cranbrook feel "left behind."

Cranbrook's modern-day economy rests on an affluent and mobile middle class, attracted by a concentration of high-performing state and private schools. The Parish's proximity to London, the prevalence of second-home ownership, the wholesale financialisation of the UK's housing markets, and the lack of new housing means the affordability gap has been stretched to the breaking point. At 19:1, the ratio of average house price to average household income makes the Parish one of the least affordable in the country. Young people who have grown up in the Parish cannot afford to stay. The majority of those working in the town or on the land are priced out and forced to commute long distances from cheaper areas.

Empowering communities to reimagine their place. The 2011 Localism Act granted new powers to communities in cities and rural villages to shape their own futures and to draw up formal Neighbourhood Development Plans (NDP). The momentum of the

CLT movement and national lobbying prompted one government minister to say "there should be a CLT in every Neighbourhood Plan." With over 1000 plans, this presented a real opportunity for growth. The implicit political message of "make your own plan, then do your own development" was just what people in Cranbrook had in mind.

In 2015, residents of Cranbrook recognized that the town needed a regeneration strategy, a body to curate it, and investment funding to make it happen. In 2017, the Council launched an NDP. A dedicated team of community volunteers also came together to initiate a CLT, so that one could support the other. The proposal to set up the Crane Valley Land Trust was backed by 500 signatures of support. Since its formation, the Land Trust has worked hand-in-hand with the NDP Steering Committee and also engaged local land owners, house builders, and potential joint-venture development partners, looking to provide the genuinely and permanently affordable housing that Cranbrook needs. A local apple grower has recently donated one acre (0.6 hectares) of land on which can be built twenty-two prototype Passivhaus homes for the community, whilst also enabling his farm manager to live on site. The homes will be affordable not only to rent or buy, but also to operate.

The challenge for Cranbrook, as with many other 'left behind' communities, is to take back control of its destiny. This is what it is doing through its NDP and the Crane Valley Land Trust, promoting sustainable housing development in policy and practical actions. The Land Trust is embodying the essential qualities and character of the town and surrounding historic rural landscape in its approach to development and as an exemplar for others to follow.

Establishing Enabling Hubs and City–CLT Partnerships[25]

The Community Housing Fund created an opportunity to build on the achievements of the first-generation Umbrella CLTs and to realise the National CLT Network's vision; that is, to develop sub-regional Enabling Hubs as support bodies for all forms of community-led housing that cover most of England with a mix of urban and rural hubs.[26] They are connected with one another in order to pool resources and to share technical expertise.

CLT East operates across the extended geography of eastern England, and is the first to have made the crossover from rural to urban political settings. One of its first successes was the project developed by the Stretham & Wilburton CLT, based on the CLT's partnership with a parish council and the East Cambridgeshire District Council. This partnership has resulted in 70 new homes, including 25 CLT homes, in a village that had previously resisted any new housing. As a result of the project, the Council developed a planning policy for enabling community-led development, and formed Palace Green Homes, a new council-owned housing development company, with part of its remit to serve as a development partner for CLTs.

A further effect of this policy innovation has been the strong support now being given to CLTs from the mayor of the recently established Cambridgeshire and Peterborough

Combined Authority, which covers an area containing those two cities as well as a range of smaller "left behind" towns, all of which may grow rapidly in the years ahead.

What is needed? The particular strength of an Enabling Hub is its understanding of the pipeline of groups and projects, and their supply chains, in a particular area. This is helpful to councils when they are attempting to get an accurate picture of the level and type of local demand, and how the council might help to meet it. Because Enabling Hubs need to operate over a wide area, and with enough volume of business to pay their way, there is an opportunity to collaborate when groups in different geographies are going through similar development processes. Collaboration is particularly valuable in urban areas where multiple groups can share in the development of a single large site or can cooperate in getting better value from local builders or off-site manufacturers.

Partnerships are key to an Enabling Hub's success. Partners may host the Hub's office functions, share staff members, and bring financial or technical support. Given that housing development can take many years, Hubs need to diversify income streams outside of project-related fees. Research may offer extra income, and help position a Hub as a

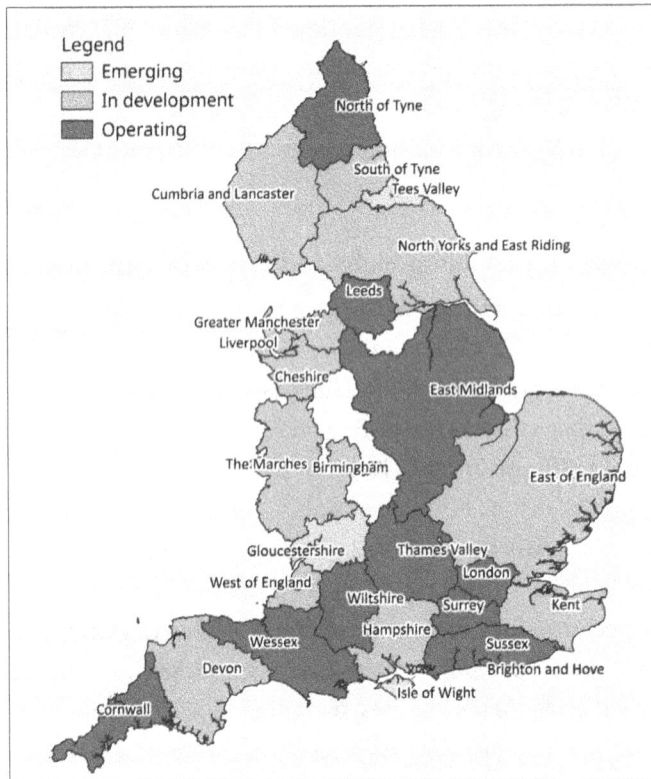

Fig. 3.3. Regions covered by the Enabling Hubs for community-led housing, as of June 2019.

thought leader in a particular area. The Oxford Hub, for example, has conducted research on the Oxford Housing Market[27] and Wessex Community Assets has conducted research on the "motivations and aspirations" of CLT volunteers in Somerset, Devon, and Dorset.[28] There are also opportunities to charge for developing and delivering training courses for prospective homebuyers, employees of local authorities and housing associations, and professionals in design, finance, and law who may have little experience working with community groups.

A new breed of civic partnerships: CLTs and City Regions. Three innovative CLTs have led the growth of city-region Enabling Hubs:

- Leeds Community Homes is a CLT created from the initiative of experienced local community-led housing organisations that had been active in the city for several decades. The CLT engages in the direct delivery of housing, funded in part through community share offers, and supports the development of other CLH organisations across the city-region.

- Bristol CLT has been a national leader in delivering innovative community-led housing projects for almost two decades. The Bristol City Council is now an integral partner of the Hub, and is offering sites to encourage the development of CLT homes and other forms of CLH.

- Oxfordshire CLT, established in 2004, had struggled to build a pipeline of projects due to the competition for sites in the highest value area in the UK, and the lack of local government support. However, the creation of the Community Housing Fund in 2016 prompted a surge of new rural and urban projects and renewed interest from the five Oxfordshire councils. In 2017, the Oxfordshire CLT forged an Enabling Hub partnership with a local philanthropic foundation and a community development charity. The CLT now focuses on holding land and partnering with smaller CLTs and other developers, rather than doing housing development on its own.

The political significance of Enabling Hubs and the wider community-led housing approach. There is no doubt that CLTs have benefited from being part of a bigger community-led housing landscape. CLTs have recognised this and have taken the lead, nationally and locally, in building community-led housing sectoral alliances — both in their own self-interest and for the survival and growth of community-led housing in general.

A handful of urban councils, moreover, have used CLTs as a response to the challenges of reduced funding from central government to maintain a supply of genuinely and permanently affordable housing. Alongside the call by CLTs for a new politics of shared control between politicians and citizens, there is now a significant potential for greater citizen involvement and community ownership of assets in urban regeneration, as a counterweight to the acceptance of regeneration as driven solely by the financial motivations of real estate developers, investors and councils.

IV. CONCLUSION: WHAT ARE CLTs REALLY ABOUT?

There are now over 300 CLTs in England and 935 CLT homes have been built. Recent research suggests there are more than 5,000 new CLT homes in the pipeline. Nationwide, the membership of CLTs has grown to over 17,000 people.

In May 2019, central government called for new information on the number of additional CLH homes that might start before 2024, to provide evidence of demand that could be met if the Community House Fund were extended beyond March 2020. Over 16,000 further CLH homes are now in prospect. Most of these are CLT homes.

The recognized impact and widespread awareness of CLTs, once distant ambitions, are increasingly visible in national and local policy making. Very few people now look puzzled when CLTs are mentioned. Familiar barriers remain, including lack of access to land, finance, and technical support, but persistent and united action by varied CLH actors is making steady progress in reducing these constraints on future development.

In June 2019, the central government reacted positively to sustained campaigns by both the CLT and Cohousing Networks to secure exemptions from potentially damaging leasehold reforms. For instance, new CLTs would have been prevented from using ground leases to protect the affordability of their homes, but they will now be "totally exempt" from any legislative changes.

The interest in CLTs as instruments for the regeneration of public housing estates, which had been proposed but abandoned in the early 2000s, is being revived. After a decade in which estate residents were excluded from decision-making by their council landlords and displaced through gentrification caused by council and developer partnerships, the political, social, and economic damage has been recognised. Councils previously hostile to community action are now working with residents on co-production for estate regeneration, with some of the new homes likely to be owned by a CLT.

The UK's main political parties are now openly endorsing CLTs. Labour's 2019 report, *Land for the Many,* argues that community land trusts should be given a greater role in alleviating the country's housing crisis.[29] A Conservative think tank has recently proposed that the estate affected by the terrible fire at Grenfell Tower should be transferred into CLT ownership.

What CLTs are really about? At the Royal Society Symposium in 1998, mentioned at the start of this chapter, housing was described as "like living, like life itself . . . messy." At the 2nd International Festival of Social Housing in Lyons, France, hosted twenty-one years later by Housing Europe, the mood was angrier and more focussed on the misuse of urban land and housing as a global speculative commodity. The potentially dire consequences for both rural and urban populations, for those at the margins, and for the now threatened middle classes, are well expressed in the catchphrase from this 2019 event: "What oil was to the industrial age, urban land is to global financial capitalism."[30]

Given the conspicuous failure of government policy and the private market to create well-ordered and fair land and housing markets that respond to needs and demand, an active citizenship is needed to refocus political attention on some fundamentals: what all citizens need; what all citizens can afford; and what all citizens should be able to afford.

Today is a time when new institutions of local democratic control are urgently needed to bring people together around issues that matter to everyone, especially the security of their homes and the cost of shelter. The communities that have done the hard work of setting up new institutions like CLTs have done so

> The task of citizens seeking their own housing solutions is not to become part of the mainstream, but to reshape the mainstream.

with a passion because they represent important political ideas about the way they want to live. These ideas belong to neither "right" nor "left." They put communities in a healthier situation than before, with better quality and genuinely affordable homes, and a real sense of identity and autonomy.

In John E. Davis' wise words, CLTs are not only "problem solving," they are "problem defining." CLTs embody an approach in which citizens can take the time to explore and to understand the complexity of their villages, towns, cities, and communities, and what makes them work. CLTs do not avoid the issues that everyone else seems determined to ignore when using a meaningless political term like "affordable housing," namely the cost of land and the stewardship of public and private land to serve the common good.

The statutory language defining CLTs in England and Wales was drafted with that participatory, problem-defining, problem-solving approach to community development in mind. Implicit in that definition is a recognition of power . . . who has it and what can be done with it. The task of citizens seeking their own housing solutions is not to become part of the mainstream, but to reshape the mainstream.

The "trick" in the design of the Community Housing Fund was to create a national policy based on local support frameworks that enable different things to happen in different places. CLTs can only realistically mobilise as a credible force to counter the global financialisation of land and housing if they can develop viable and credible alternatives of many different kinds that are adapted to and appropriate to their communities and their places. Global change happens through local intelligence, innovation, and action.

Messy is both good . . . and necessary!

2021 POSTSCRIPT:
CAN MESSY BE TRANSFORMATIVE?

Tom Chance

Like many ex-mining towns, Dinnington in South Yorkshire has high unemployment and low life expectancy. Obesity—especially in children—is above average and there are no designated sport and leisure facilities in the town. There are almost no community facilities. It's what UK policy heads now call a "left behind town"—though few people in such places would welcome the label.

In the space of just five years, local residents have created a plan to turn things around and have set up a community land trust to make it happen. They're starting by building 30 homes for low rents on a piece of land abandoned for over 20 years. But they plan to go on and build more homes, regenerate the town centre, build more community and sports facilities, and improve the local green spaces. They want to do everything!

Such ambition defies the British instinct that a "left behind" community needs lots of top-down interventions. But the community's early success has been made possible because the national Government introduced neighbourhood planning in the 2011 Localism Act, and created the Community Housing Fund off the back of the CLT Network's lobbying in 2018.

One way of seeing these policies is as building blocks for community action. Brick by brick, the movement is building itself up.

Dinnington CLT can be — in the policy parlance — a "new market entrant," diversifying the housebuilding market in the town and building additional homes that wouldn't otherwise get built. This is very much how the UK Government sees the CLT movement: a useful niche adding some homes on the fringes of the market.

By the summer of 2021, there were 327 fully formed CLTs, with as many as 200 more in various stages of formation. They had built or renovated 1,100 homes, and owned another 640. So we can talk of steady progress in building this niche in the face of considerable barriers.

But another way of seeing the Dinnington CLT story is of transformation. What if the CLT is able not just to carve out a niche in the town, but to be the driving force of its renewal? What if the community is not just given scraps of land for small development projects, but is able to partner on equal terms with local government and the private sector on any and all residential, commercial, and recreational developments in the town?

What is stopping this from happening?

The story of another town couldn't be more different. On the south coast of England in prosperous Kent, Ashford is a nexus for high speed rail within the UK and to the rest of Europe. The town is growing fast.

The Ashford council has led the development of a new "garden community" of

5,750 homes on its southern edge in a development called Chilmington Green. The scheme is governed by a partnership of four private developers, borough and county councils, the Government's main housing delivery agency, Homes England, and a local business partnership. So far — and so familiar — the only role for the community was through a community stakeholder group which met bi-monthly with the council and lead developer.

But look closer and it's more interesting. The council set up the long-term management and stewardship body as a Community Management Organisation, with a legal structure that is in effect a CLT. Residents can join as members, vote for the Board, and have seats on the Board. The company is set up for the wellbeing of the community and can only use its assets for those purposes. It will take on ownership of the public space and community facilities, which will generate revenues to sustain its work. While the four developers have a blocking 50% vote on the Board for now, once the development is complete they will drop away and be replaced by resident members.

What is going on here? Why have the councils and developers not grasped that this is essentially a CLT and promoted it as such, harking back to Letchworth and the story told in Chapter One of this monograph? Lifting our gaze from Ashford to the whole of the UK, why has the Town and Country Planning Association had so little success in promoting community ownership and stewardship as the top two principles for new garden communities?

One other development of note in the past year could easily be missed. A housing association, which can't yet be named, has applied to become a Strategic Partner of Homes England. This boils down to being given one big pot of money to get on and build, rather than applying for grants for each development it takes forward. For the first time, Homes England asked applicants to state how the partnership would enable more development with CLTs. And this housing association has put CLTs at the heart of its strategy.

This exemplifies a recommendation by Danny Kruger MP, in a report commissioned by the Prime Minister, that partnerships between CLTs and housing associations should be the future of social housing provision in England. A right-leaning think tank, *Onward*, has made a similar suggestion, and influential figures in our housing sector like Lord Best have called for the same. They echo the suggestions in the mid-2000s for CLTs underpinning housing association-led regeneration mentioned by Stephen Hill, Catherine Harrington, and Tom Archer in their original essay.

After 15 years of successful partnership schemes, and this increasing level of political endorsement, why is this model still on the sidelines? Why are the vast majority of housing associations ignoring CLTs, or even lobbying against our movement?

The answer to these questions — i.e., what is stopping CLTs taking a leading role like in Dinnington? what is stopping large government or developer-initiated schemes from being set up as CLTs? what is stopping the mainstream adoption of CLT partnerships by housing associations?—lies in the deep-rooted culture of paternalism in the UK.

In our national mindset, we simply don't believe that community ownership and stewardship can scale, and can ever be on a par with government, large private developers, or the large corporate housing associations.

In too many cases, CLTs succeed *in spite of* government and the market, rather than policy and market structures facilitating and nurturing the power of community.

So the Community Housing Fund—hugely successful, as described in the preceding essay—ran for just 18 months outside London and then closed. The Government allowed community-led housing projects with over 10,000 homes in the works languish for over a year, until finally announcing a token £4 million to re-open the Fund with what looks to be a six-month window to bid for the cash and then spend it.

The UK Government is happy to support CLTs in order to get some additional homes built in niche contexts. It was willing, after a lot of work on the Network's part, to include an exemption from a ban on ground rents in a bill laid before Parliament. But the Government doesn't treat the CLT movement or community-led housing with the kind of consistency that is required of any half-decent industrial strategy. They aren't backing the sector to allow it to scale up.

The messiness of the CLT movement in the UK has created room for boundless innovation and remarkable examples. But it is slow to touch mainstream practice, outside of a few exceptional councils and housing associations. This is the biggest challenge for our movement.

Stephen, Catherine and Tom looked back over the ten years since the formation of the National CLT Network and saw remarkable progress.

Ten years from now, will we look back on another decade of messy and steady progress, resulting in, say, 600 CLTs initiated by grassroots communities with a collective portfolio of 3,000 homes? Or, in 2031, will we be talking about a *transformation* in the culture of government and industry, with CLTs seen as an important component of the tool box for the regeneration of towns, the development of large new communities, and the building and regeneration of social housing?

I would be proud to have played a part in either story. But the latter informs our larger mission. The Network's ultimate, transformative goal is to *mainstream* the community ownership of affordable housing and land.

—

Acknowledgments: Our thanks go to five people who contributed to this chapter: Pat Conaty, Kate Braithwaite, Kirsty Tait, Charlie Fisher, and Tim Kemp, all of whom have played or are still playing significant roles in the English CLT story. They each provided a distinctive and valid perspective of key events. Please excuse any minor discrepancies in joining up all the threads of that story, in the spirit of creative and productive messiness.

Notes

1. CLTs in England are concerned primarily with the provision of permanently and genuinely affordable housing that is retained in community ownership and control. Affordability is defined by reference to official Area Median Income data or local equivalents, with the traditional measure of one-third of household income being spent on housing costs. CLTs own land freehold or on very long leases, usually for 250 years or more. They either develop and own the homes directly, or they grant leases to other regulated affordable housing providers to build homes on their behalf on lease terms that maintain appropriate community controls. Council estate regeneration CLTs were also predicated on CLTs owning the freehold of the land, with other housing providers developing under leases. CLT homes may be either ownership or rental. Over the period covered by the chapter, CLTs in England became more focussed on rental housing as the economic and employment conditions for sustainable homeownership became increasingly difficult. Some CLTs have expanded from their original focus on housing to own other assets for community benefit. The Butchers Arms public house, rescued by the Lyvennet CLT in Cumbria, is one example: *http://www.thebutchersarms.pub*

2. Contributed by Pat Conaty, a Fellow at the New Economics Foundation. He was part of the Community Finance Solutions team whose research and advocacy led to the CLT Fund and the CLT National Demonstration Project.

3. See: *https://papers.ssrn.com/sol3/papers.cfm?abstract_id=1128862*

4. CDFIs are loan funds that emerged in the USA in the 1970s to support non-bankable but viable enterprises. One of the first was the Revolving Loan Fund created by the Institute for Community Economics in the USA that funded the early CLTs and was an inspiration for CDFIs in the UK.

5. Contributed by Dr. Kate Braithwaite and Kirsty Tait. Dr. Kate Braithwaite has served as CEO of Cumbria's Rural Community Council, Director of Carnegie UK Trust's Rural Programme, and Operations Director at UnLtd—the Foundation for Social Entrepreneurs. Kirsty Tait currently works for the Scottish Land Commission. She was previously on staff at the Carnegie UK Trust, where she supported English CLT pioneers and the set-up of the National CLT Network.

6. The Carnegie UK Trust was instrumental in providing financial support for this work.

7. Paterson, B and Dayson, K, *Proof of Concept: Community Land Trusts.* A Community Finance Solutions, University of Salford (2011, p. 13).

8. Further documentation relating to this aspect of CLT development is available in an archive of primary and secondary source materials compiled by Stephen Hill, Catherine Hand, and Graham Moody at: *https://independent.academia.edu/StephenHill3*

9. "Growth Areas" were designated by central government as part of its Sustainable Communities Plan to tackle the decline of urban centres in the North and Midlands, while creating new communities in response to demand in the South and East.

10. Developers mostly treated this as a box-ticking formality to secure a planning permission.

11. The Foundation's founder, Joseph Rowntree, had an interest in land and its role in the political economy of nations. He was an enthusiast for Henry George's writing on land and for Ebenezer Howard's Garden Cities. In 1902, Rowntree started building a garden village at New Earswick, in York, as "a rightly ordered and self-governing community."

12. See: *https://www.jrf.org.uk/report/land-housing-current-practice-and-future-options*

13. An NDC in Sunderland is a good example. Still controlled by the community, it owns and develops affordable housing and is continuing to improve the area and to generate income.

14. Members of the Institute of Community Economics had talked about DSNI during a visit to London in the early 2000s.

15. Included on this board was Stephen Hill, a co-author of the present chapter.

16. Aird, J. (2009). *Lessons from the first 150 Homes: Evaluation of the National Community Land Trust Demonstration Programme 2006–2008.* Salford, CFS. Nineteen CLTs are listed on page 25, incorporated as of 2008, but Stonesfield CLT was omitted.

17. Aird, J. (2009). Ibid.

18. In 2011, the National CLT Network took over the administration of the seed corn grants, thereafter called the "CLT Start Up Fund," working with the original charitable foundation donors. The Fund closed in 2020. The loans continue as the main CLT Fund, administered and funded by the Charities Aid Foundation, with Charity Bank.

19. Aird, J. (2009). Ibid.

20. 45 CLTs had adopted the Wessex housing association partnership model, and 9 CLTs had themselves become a housing association or Registered Provider, regulated by government to own and manage social rent homes. All these CLTs, and some in the process of registration, would have been affected by the 2015 Housing and Planning Bill.

21. Tenant Management Organisations (resident management of publicly owned social rent housing) and Self-Help Housing (bringing empty homes back into use and community ownership) were also engaged to create a diverse and expanding CLH sector. The definition of "Community-Led Housing" adopted by government as qualifying criteria for receiving grants or loans from the Community Housing Fund (2016–2020) draws

heavily on the CLT statutory definition. (1) Meaningful community engagement and consent occurs throughout the process. The community does not necessarily have to initiate and manage the development process, or build the homes themselves, although many may do so. (2) The local community group or organisation owns, manages, or stewards the homes in a manner of their choosing. (3) The benefits to the local area and/or specified community must be clearly defined and legally protected in perpetuity.

22. Community Led Homes is a formal alliance of the four main CLH bodies, channelling communication, advocacy and support through a single "brand:" National CLT Network leads on developing the Enabling Hub infrastructure; Confederation of Co-operative Housing leads the training and accreditation of enablers and technical advisers; UK Cohousing Network provides a single point of access, the National Advice Centre, for all types of CLH, curates the Community Led Homes website, and manages its library of technical resources; and Locality, a national membership network for community asset owning organisations, which manages a small grants programme for areas not yet covered by Enabling Hubs. The National CLT Network holds the Government contract.

23. Archer, T. Green, S. and Fisher, C. (2019). Helping Communities Build. *https://www.cafonline.org/about-us/blog-home/venturesome-blog/helping-communities-build*

24. Contributed by Timp Kemp, a co-founder of the Crane Valley Land Trust in 2017. He was Chairman of Cranbrook & Sissinghurst Parish Council Neighbourhood Development Plan steering committee 2015–2016 and Vice-Chair until May 2019.

25. Contributed by Charlie Fisher, a director of Transition by Design. He has been a trustee of the Oxfordshire CLT since 2013 and was part of the set-up team for a new Thames Valley Enabling Hub.

26. Some enabling hubs have emerged from the Action with Communities in Rural England (ACRE) Network.

27. See: *https://issuu.com/cohohub/docs/oxfordclh_finalreport_and_appendice*

28. See: *http://wessexca.co.uk/wp-content/uploads/2016/06/3016725-Wessex-Report.pdf*

29. *Land for the Many: Changing the Way Our Fundamental Asset Is Used, Owned, and Governed* (June 2019): *https://landforthemany.uk*

30. See: *http://www.housingeurope.eu/blog-1283/access-to-affordable-and-adquate-housing-is-perhaps-the-social-problem-of-our-generation#.XP-W70XcHlI.twitter*

4.

From Pressure Group to Government Partner

The Story of the Brussels Community Land Trust

Geert De Pauw and Nele Aernouts

A housing crisis has been raging in the Brussels Capital Region for decades. The failure of government to address this problem prompted neighborhood associations and housing rights activists in Brussels to join forces in 2008 and to look for solutions of their own. In their search, they stumbled upon an Anglo-Saxon model that had remained largely unnoticed in the European mainland: the community land trust. It seemed to comprise everything they were looking for.

In 2013, the Community Land Trust Brussels (CLTB) was established and received support from the regional government. The first newly constructed CLT homes were inhabited in 2015, and new housing projects are now being built at various locations in Brussels. Meanwhile, CLTB has been playing an important role in disseminating the CLT model in Europe.

In this chapter, we will provide an overview of the housing crisis in Brussels. We will then discuss the origins of the Brussels CLT. Starting the CLT was relatively quick and easy, but the road to putting the organization on a firm footing has not been without challenges. From the beginning, CLTB has had to cope with a number of legal, organisational, and institutional barriers. We will discuss some of these struggles and the agreements put in place to resolve them, before concluding with a look at future prospects for CLT growth in Brussels.

I. WELCOME TO BRUSSELS, CAPITAL OF EUROPE!

The implementation of a CLT in the Brussels Capital Region can only be understood within the context of the region's chronic housing problems. For several decades, a substantial fraction of the housing stock has been unaffordable for a considerable share of the population. A severe mismatch between average household incomes and average housing prices is at the core of the problem: for half of households living in Brussels, the share of their household budget going to pay for housing exceeds 40% (Romainville, 2009). This problem, which academics and housing activists have come to term a "housing crisis," is based on several dichotomies and inadequate policy responses.

A Socio-Economic Dichotomy

Since the restructuring of the labor market in the 1980s, the Brussels Capital Region has been marked by considerable economic growth. This growth has been driven by the service sector, which is dominated by European, federal, and regional administrations and has attracted international and multi-national corporations (Loopmans & Kesteloot, 2009).

This economic growth is not entirely to the benefit of the population residing within Brussels, nor are the benefits of growth shared evenly among them. Here are a few indications. Half of the jobs in the Brussels Capital Region (BCR) are held by inhabitants of Belgium's two other regions, Wallonia and Flanders, who commute into Brussels on a daily basis. Among all of the regions in Europe, the BCR is ranked 4th in Gross Domestic Product (GDP),[1] but it is ranked 145th when it comes to the disposable household income of BCR's population (Englert et al., 2018). The BCR also exhibits a pattern of high levels of poverty and large numbers of people on welfare. The percentage of BCR's population who are at risk of poverty is significantly higher than in Belgium's other regions: 39% of the Brussels population is at risk of poverty, compared to 27% in Wallonia and 14% in Flanders.[2] At least 23% of the children in Brussels are growing up in households in which no income is earned through the job market (Englert et al., 2018).

An External and Internal Migration Dichotomy

Another dichotomy can be identified when looking at external and internal migration patterns, fueled by different streams of migration following World War II. Among all inhabitants of the Brussels Capital Region, 35% of them have a non-Belgian nationality, while 72% have non-Belgian origins.[3] On the one side of the spectrum, every expansion of the EU brings highly skilled EU migrants and an increased attractiveness for foreign corporations and new highly skilled migrants (Englert et al., 2018). On the other side, the migration waves of the 1960s and 1970s brought mainly Moroccan and Italian guest workers, few of whom were able to climb the social ladder due to the economic crises of the mid-1970s and 1980s. Later on, these immigrants were joined by family members and a more diverse group of new immigrants. They have often ended up in informal or low-paid economic circuits, such as the building, cleaning, transport and catering sectors (Loopmans & Kesteloot, 2008).

Spatially, the high-skilled native and foreign populations have settled in peripheral municipalities, while lower-income groups have found housing in the more central, post-industrial neighborhoods of Brussels along the Canal, an area known as the "poor crescent" (Kesteloot, 2000).[4] For decades, this area has been dealing with severe problems of housing quality that range from moisture problems to a lack of heating systems, and to phenomena such as overcrowding and subletting (Englert et al., 2018). In more recent years, problems of affordability have also emerged.

Inadequate Policy Responses

Public policy has historically given an inadequate answer to these dichotomies. From its very inception, Belgian housing policy has been marked by an anti-urban attitude, represented by a persistent priority for stimulating homeownership outside of the cities. Spatial planning policies, meanwhile, have been nearly absent (Dedecker, 2008).

Belgian housing policy has had its greatest impact on the residential movements of upwardly mobile families, supporting homeownership outside of cities through fiscal grants and cheap railway tickets. From the 1950s onward, families in search of a green, less-dense environment were helped to buy houses in the peripheries outside the Brussels Capital Region. This focus on homeownership didn't change fundamentally after the regionalization of the nation's housing policy.[5] Today, half of the region's housing budget goes to supporting homeownership, a policy intended to keep middle-class households within the BCR and, simultaneously, to increase tax revenues. This public support for homeownership takes the form of tax deductions,[6] soft mortgages,[7] and direct grants for the development of housing serving homeowners with modest incomes.[8] Such development has often been concentrated in the "poor crescent," in order to increase the area's "social mix" and to create a domino effect of attracting further private investment.[9]

> The amount of social housing is stuck at 7.5%, even though half of the population qualifies for social housing.

Despite taking such a large share of the housing policy budget, the homeownership rate has declined during the last decades, due primarily to a steep rise in housing prices.[10] Furthermore, among the beneficiaries of this homeownership policy, middle-income households are overrepresented. These households enjoy the benefit of this "extra encouragement," but are not necessarily in need of additional funding to become homeowners (Dessouroux et al., 2016, p.24).

The persistent focus on conventional, market-priced homeownership has impeded the growth of community-based housing and creation of a decent social rental market (Geurts and Goossens, 2004). Today, the amount of social housing is stuck at 7.5%, even though half of the BCR's population qualifies for social housing (Englert et al., 2018). Due to the small amount of social housing, there is excessive demand in the private rental market, which allows landlords to impose strict requirements for the selection of tenants. Not surprisingly, these requirements are characterized by discrimination and racism, especially targeting prospective tenants with a social assistance benefit or a disability benefit and/or those having a particular ethnic background (Heylen & Van den Broeck, 2015). The BCR launched several programs to build additional social housing, but very few homes have been constructed and the impact on the housing crisis has been close to zero.

Urban policies and programs aimed at the redevelopment of inner-city neighborhoods have been inadequate at best and harmful at worst, with regard to affordable housing. (Dessouroux et al., 2016). For decades after putting into effect the 1953 slum-clearing law (*Wet op de Krotopruiming*) and high-rise replacements of the 1960s and 1970s, no decent urban renewal program was developed to address the deterioration of under-privileged areas. Deindustrialization in the Belgian economy left these neighborhoods with a deteriorating housing stock, poor-quality public spaces and an impoverished, transient and aging population. Not until 1993, with the introduction of "neighbor-hood contracts" by the Brussels government, did public policy begin to tackle these problems. These "contracts" enhanced local regeneration through investment in pub-lic spaces and services, programs to promote social-economic integration, renovations of buildings, and the construction of housing on residual parcels (Vermeulen, 2009).

Two additional policies for territorial development, the Regional Zoning Plan (2012) and the International Development Plan (2018), focused on revitalization of the area and the development of housing along the Canal.

The urban policies of the past twenty-five years have been widely praised for tak-ing a more integrated and inclusionary approach to neighborhood development and for explicitly addressing the social-spatial fragmentation of Brussels. But there has also been a darker, less praiseworthy side to these policies. The reservation of large lands for redevelopment by private investors and the repeated mantra in government policies and plans of needing a better "social mix" in inner-city neighborhoods have had an implicit aim: attracting higher-income groups to these areas. As public and private investment increases, however, land values and housing prices rise, making it harder for lower-in-come people to gain access to affordable housing.

In sum, the benefits of economic growth in the Brussels Capital Region have been inequitably shared across geographic areas and across social classes. Patterns of gentrifica-tion have been supported by a housing and urban policy promoting the revitalization of inner-city neighborhoods. These economic and social realities, combined with a housing system fraught with problems of deterioration, discrimination, unaffordability, and the meagre production of social housing, eventually pushed concerned activists and com-munity organizations into the housing domain, seeking alternatives to forms of housing provided by either the state or the market.

II. CREATION OF THE BRUSSELS COMMUNITY LAND TRUST

In 2007, the "Ministry of Housing Crisis," a grassroots initiative launched by squatters, homeless people, community organizations, and housing activists, occupied the empty Gesu Monastery in Sint Joost to call attention to the housing problem. In addition to ini-tiatives asking the government to take responsibility for the housing crisis, there were also experiments with new solutions. For instance, the community center, Bonnevie, initiated l'Espoir in the municipality of Molenbeek with the support of CIRE, an association that mainly works with refugees and newcomers. CIRE had previously developed solidarity savings groups, where low-income families collectively save money to finance the purchase of individual homes. The l'Espoir housing project produced fourteen affordable, energy-efficient, owner-occupied homes. The low-income families who purchased these homes were closely involved in the project's development, right from the start. Through design workshops, they influenced the building plans, they started a savings group to prepare for the purchase of the homes, and they became an important partner in discussions during the building process, alongside Fonds du Logement (the developer), the architect, and the municipality (De Pauw, 2011).

The l'Espoir housing project successfully linked a dimension of collective endeavor and solidarity to individual homeownership. However, the sponsors realized that the classic homeownership formula used in this project did not provide a structural solution for the housing crisis. The project required substantial subsidies from government to make it work, which would be lost whenever the homes were subsequently resold. Nor were there guarantees against future speculation. The project's sponsors started looking for an alternative strategy that would make the homes permanently affordable and would structurally integrate resident participation into the design and operation of the housing.

In the United States they discovered the CLT model, which was largely unknown on the European mainland until then. In September 2009, the British Building and Social Housing Foundation (named World Habitat today) invited four community developers from Brussels to take part in an international study visit to the Champlain Housing Trust in Burlington, Vermont.[11] After a week, the group returned to Brussels convinced that the CLT model was what they were looking for. During a conference on cooperative housing in Brussels, they publicly launched the plan to start campaigning for the creation of a CLT in Brussels, which was received with great interest.

This eventually led to a charter for the establishment of the Community Land Trust Brussels. The charter was signed on May 25, 2010 by fifteen associations. During three public meetings, the concept was explained and discussed with the participants: families in need of housing, community organizers, housing rights activists, and academics interested in the model. Hundreds of people participated in these events, while a small core group met regularly to set out a strategy and to seek further support for the plan. Out of this dynamic, the Platform Community Land Trust Brussels, the precursor of the Brussels CLT, eventually grew.[12] The Platform, a group of supportive organisations, set itself the aim of promoting the CLT model in Brussels. The organization's leaders wrote a few articles about their ideas, talked to the press, and arranged a series of trainings, lectures, film performances, and public assemblies to explain the model. They started to develop scenarios for the establishment of a CLT in Brussels and to search for subsidies to make this happen. In 2011, the Green Minister for Housing of the Brussels Capital Region

commissioned a feasibility study. The recommendations of the study were put into practice in 2012 and led to establishment of the actual community land trust.

In Brussels, the CLT is composed of two bodies, a nonprofit association and a Foundation. Both were officially founded in 2012. The Region granted a subsidy covering
the costs of development for CLTB's first housing project. Financial support from the
Brussels Capital Region enabled CLTB to start constructing dwellings that could be
made affordable for the lowest income groups soon after its formation. Monies from the
government also financed the creation of a team of four people who started working for
CLTB in September 2012.

In 2013, community land trusts were included in the Brussels' Housing Code.[13] The
Code mentioned CLTs alongside existing tools such as social rental housing and social
mortgages. It defined what CLTs are and stated that the government could define, in an
implementing law, the rules according to which CLTs could get recognized by the Region.
To date, this law hasn't been drafted, but the fact that CLTs were quoted in the Code had
an important symbolical function.

In 2014, the government secured the financing of CLT operations by including CLTB
as a participant in the Housing Alliance. This investment program for new affordable
housing in the Brussels region ensured that 2 million euros could be invested each year
between 2014 and 2018 for the development of new CLT projects. CLTB could use this
money for the acquisition of land and for covering a part of the construction costs.

Early Projects

Together with local partner associations, CLTB has created a development pipeline of
twelve projects to date. Most of them are located in neighborhoods of the "poor crescent,"
adding to an "in situ" regeneration of these areas. These projects include a total of more
than 180 dwellings and six spaces for community infrastructure. Almost all of the projects are multi-family homes. The first CLTB project, *l'Ecluse* (9 homes), has been inhabited since 2015. Five new projects are in construction; five others are being prepared.

The *Arc-en-Ciel* project in Molenbeek, the largest project until now, is one of CLTB's
flagships. The vacant land that used to include a house and workshop was bought in 2013.
However, due to several delays within the construction process, notably for obtaining the
building permit, it took more than six years to build *Arc-en-Ciel*. Together with the Housing Fund,[14] a social housing agency, and several partner associations, CLTB developed
32 dwellings, a community garden, and a women's community center on this land. Since
the very beginning, the future residents have been intensively involved in the project's
development, participating in architecture workshops, assemblies, and general meetings.
Construction was completed at the end of 2019 and the homeowners began moving into
their new homes.

A kilometer away, in the municipality of Anderlecht, an old Parish Centre is being

Fig 4.1. l'Ecluse, CLTB's first homes. MARC DETIFFE

transformed into seven owner-occupied homes, a community garden, and a building for a neighborhood association. This project was also launched in 2013. The group of future residents was composed that same year. They called their project *Le Nid*, which means "the Nest." Like *Arc-en-Ciel*, construction was completed in the summer of 2019.

The *Liedts* project, which includes four senior dwellings above a service center in Schaerbeek, focuses on intergenerational living.

The most emblematic project in preparation is called CALICO. This project, constructed by a private developer, is funded by the European Union through an Urban Innovative Actions grant.[15] To obtain this funding, CLTB partnered with two cohousing groups. One of them focuses on women and gender issues, while the other aims to develop a "home for birth and end-of-life" where women can give birth and the elderly can spend their last days in a warm, homelike environment. The project consists of 34 dwellings, the home for birth and end-of-life, and a community center. It focuses on solidarity and community care and is scheduled for completion in 2021.

Finally, one single-family home deserves special mention. In a city as dense and expensive as Brussels, CLTB didn't consider single-family dwellings a possibility. It took two devoted families to convince CLTB of the contrary. An elderly couple who lived near the *l'Ecluse* CLT project was looking for a smaller, single-story dwelling that might better fit their age and family size. Their house with a garden had become too big for them to handle after their children left home. They met one of the families living in *l'Ecluse*, who was looking for a bigger home after their family had expanded. The families decided to swap homes. Doing so, the first family offered the land under the house to CLTB, in order to make it affordable for the family from *l'Ecluse* and to preserve its affordability for generations to come. CLTB hopes this example can inspire others, thus creating affordable homes without any subsidies.

III. CREATIVITY AND REFLEXIVITY

In the beginning, the idea to develop a CLT in the Brussels Capital Region was met with a lot of skepticism from housing experts and politicians. It was said that such a "North American model" could not be applied in Europe. The legal systems were too different; the gap between common law and civil law too great. Other criticisms were aimed at the residents of CLT housing. The community-led process inherent in the CLT model was said to be intertwined with an Anglo-Saxon tradition that was foreign to Belgium. The low-income groups inhabiting CLT projects would not properly take care of their homes, leading to a decrease in property values. The collectively led model would need too much public funding.

Although the Brussels CLT was established relatively quickly, the initiators had to face all of these criticisms and challenges. They were forced to apply a strong dose of creativity and reflexivity throughout their praxis in developing strategies to cope with them, beginning with the problem of legally separating ownership of the dwellings from ownership of the land.

A Bundle of Property Rights

Similar to CLTs in other countries, CLTB includes resale conditions in its land lease contracts in order to keep its homes permanently affordable. This is a renewable, fifty-year right in which CLTB gives the residents permission to own a dwelling on land that is not theirs. An owner may resell his/her property whenever he or she wants, but the resale price is limited and the CLTB will indicate to whom the property must be sold. In this way, the dwellings remain affordable without the government having to invest a second time. Owners are also not allowed to rent out their dwellings, except under certain conditions and for a social rent specified in the land lease. Otherwise, CLTB homeowners have the same rights and obligations as any other homeowner.

CLTB largely modelled its own land lease contracts, resale formulas, bylaws and regulations on those of CLTs in the United States. Integrating the North American community land trust model into the Belgian legal system was not a simple matter, however. Especially challenging was to find a legal solution to separating the ownership of land and dwellings, but this proved to be easier for CLT organizers to accomplish in Belgium than for CLT organizers in the United Kingdom, another common law country.

Belgian law includes two rights that enable the separation of land from the buildings on it: the surface right (*droit de superficie*) and the long-term lease (*bail emphytéotique*). The biggest difference between these two rights is the maximum duration, 50 years for the first and 99 years for the second. Neither can be automatically renewed and extended beyond the maximum period, presenting a potential obstacle to a CLT's commitment to preserve the permanent affordability of land and housing. That is one of the reasons these rights haven't been commonly used for housing.

There is a significant exception, though. In the early 1970s, a new university town was built in Belgium, inspired by contemporary innovations in urban planning. The city of Louvain-la-Neuve was constructed entirely on a concrete slab, separating underground car traffic and parking from overground pedestrian traffic. The land on which the university town is built is owned by the university, which leases out parcels under the principle of *bail emphytéotique*. The houses on these leaseholds are mainly owned by residents or private landlords. The leasehold contracts contain a clause that ensures that, each time a house changes hands, a new duration of 99 years begins to run. By "re-starting the clock" for each new homeowner, a leasehold comes very close to being permanent.

In Louvain-la-Neuve, however, no anti-speculative conditions were attached to the land leases.[16] The university remains the owner of the land, but it does not have the right to restrict price increases on resale of the dwellings. It is doubtful the university wanted to do so, but it is also true that it is difficult to regulate resale prices under *bail emphytéotique* due to the strong protection of property rights within Belgian law. Even if a buyer and seller were to agree to accept a number of contractual resale conditions, there would always be the risk of a court overturning them, deciding such restrictions to be in conflict with property rights.

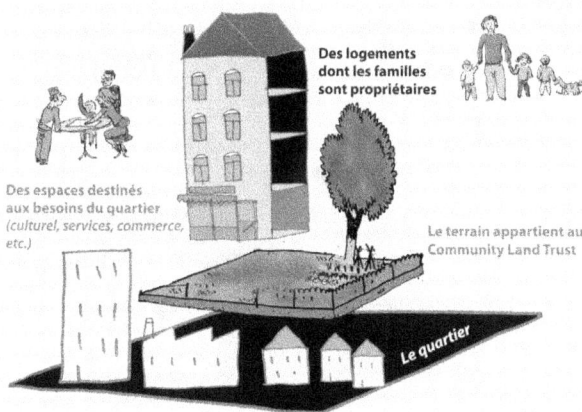

Fig 4.2. Detail of poster created by the Brussels CLT, illustrating the separate ownership of land and buildings.

It is easier to impose restrictions on the resale price, as well as other conditions concerning the use of the home, through the shorter 50-year duration of the *droit de superficie*. Therefore CLTB finally opted for the *droit de superficie*, combining clauses similar to those used in Louvain-la-Neuve with clauses, such as restricting the resale price, thereby creating a lease that is close to everlasting. This leads to fairly complex contracts. Since almost all CLTB dwellings are part of condominiums, even more conditions and variations get added to the ground lease depending on the building developer and on whether the building is renovated or newly constructed.

Undoubtedly, the government could play an important role in the future by facilitating the development of specific legislation oriented towards this variety of property regimes, specifying conditions on the use of the dwelling, the condominium, and the land on which the project is built. Such legislation could simplify the contracts and enhance the legal enforceability of the conditions.

Supporting and Strengthening the CLT Community

CLTB is composed of two closely affiliated legal entities: a nonprofit association[17] responsible for the day-to-day operations; and a public utility foundation[18] that owns the land. They are connected to each other through their bylaws. Both are run by a board of directors whose members include three groups of stakeholders: residents living in dwellings on CLTB land or waiting for a CLT home; representatives of civil society, including members of partner organizations and neighbors of CLT homes; and representatives of the Brussels government. Each stakeholder group gets one-third of the seats.[19]

In contrast to the practice of most CLTs in the United States, once people are interested in buying a house from the CLT, they must become a member of CLTB. As a member of the association, they are automatically registered on a waiting list, and are entitled to vote in electing their representatives to the managing board. Each year some hundred members gather in the general assembly to elect their representatives. These meetings are always one of the highlights of CLTB's community life.

In order to purchase a property from CLTB, households must meet the same income qualifications as required for renting in social housing. While this is a maximum income limit, CLTB is also committed to serving people whose income is even lower. To make this possible, it sets different selling prices depending on the income of the buyers. To this end, the target group is divided into four different income categories. Depending on the income category in which a homebuyer falls, he or she will pay a higher or lower price for the same type of dwelling. Homes for each of these four categories will be realized in each new project. Members on top of the waiting list get priority, according to their income category and their family size.

When launching a new housing project, future residents are selected from the waiting list and brought together in a "project group."[20] These future residents are involved in the design and preparation of the housing project and will be in charge of its management, once the dwellings are built and occupied.

It is stating the obvious that the participation of such a mixed community in the collective management of both CLTB and its projects, a community that includes professionals from ministerial cabinets, social workers, and low-income groups, can be complicated. But CLTB is convinced such a mix of interests and perspectives is essential. Through the

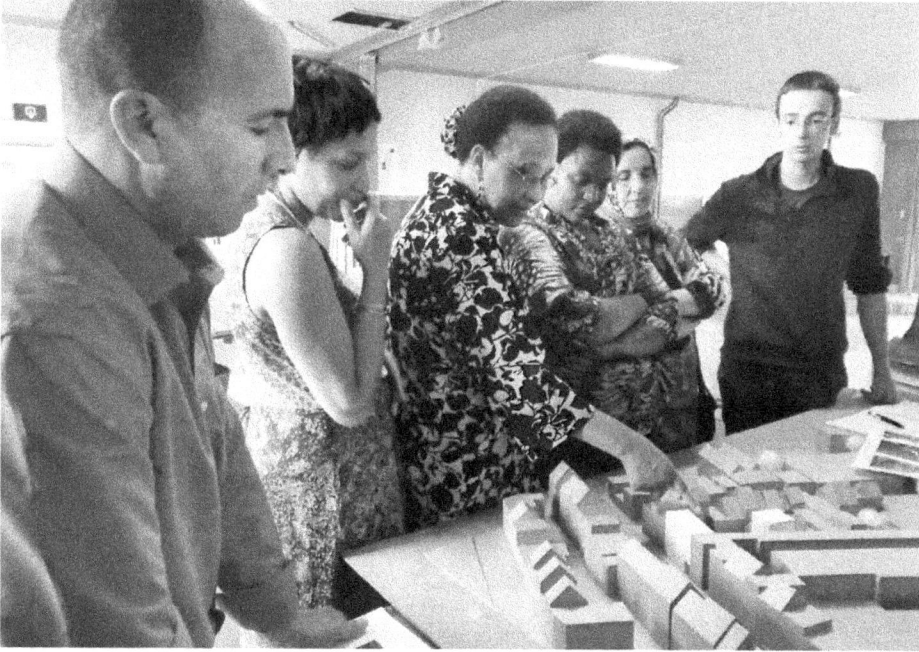

Fig 4.3. Project group for a future CLTB project, Luminiere du Nord.

participation of public officials and civil society, CLTB tries to ensure a long-term integration of public concerns and common interests, such as the integration of the dwelling within the neighborhood, the importance of affordable housing for low-income groups, and the necessity of developing a certain amount of dwellings. Similarly, the active participation of future residents, even when many of them are low-skilled and some have only a basic level of French,[21] is deemed by CLTB to be indispensable, since all decisions that are made will concern their future well-being. Once installed in their homes, they become responsible for keeping the condominium going. As condominium owners, they will have to ensure that the common charges are paid, that costs are correctly distributed, that necessary repairs are made, that a reserve fund is created, and so on. Training and guidance are key, therefore, to preparing and supporting residents in the management of their own housing.

The preparation period, which can sometimes take more than five years, is used to train residents about their legal rights and obligations; the architecture, use, and maintenance of their dwelling; and the management of a multi-unit project. To do this, CLTB collaborates with local partner organizations, who organize training sessions and individually supervise the members of the group. This leads to the establishment of important agreements and initiatives. Future residents draw up a set of rules and divide the dwellings in joint consultation; they write a charter on how they want to live together; and they take the initiative in introducing the project to people who already live in the neighborhood.

In Molenbeek, for instance, every month the *Arc-en-Ciel* group organizes the Bazar

Fig. 4.4. Annual General Meeting, Brussels CLT, 2015.

Festival on the pavement in front of the construction site of their housing project. The Bazar Festival is a festive flea market for the neighborhood. Members of the project groups have indicated how all of this helps them to acquire new skills, to cultivate self-confidence, and to strengthen the cohesion in the group (Aernouts & Ryckewaert, 2017).

Another strategy to strengthen the (future) residents and to help them in taking up their role in these different levels of management is to actively bring together the somewhat artificial CLTB community. This community is made up of approximately two hundred sympathizers and nearly four hundred families who would like someday to obtain a home through CLTB. They live in different places in the Brussels Region and usually do not know each other when they sign on as a member. They meet each other, at best, only at the annual general meeting. CLTB has now started a membership program that wants to overcome this separation and unfamiliarity among this large constituency. The program aims to strengthen both the connections among individual members and solidarity across the entire community by developing collective projects outside of the housing domain. Thanks to this program, CLTB's members have set up a group that organizes cycling lessons, they have organized the temporary use of buildings that are awaiting demolition or renovation, and they have participated in fundraising activities for CLTB.

Institutionalisation without Bureaucratization?

CLTB has grown from an informal citizens' initiative into a professional organization in just a few years. The number of dwellings produced is still limited, mainly due to the long duration of the development of real estate projects in Brussels. The plan, from now on, is to deliver twenty to thirty new homes annually. But CLTB has the ambition to increase production even further, with a goal of having a thousand dwellings on its land by 2030.

Whether this is possible will largely depend on political support and the willingness of governmental bodies to continue making funds and lands available. The growth of the organization's portfolio and CLTB's strong dependence on governmental resources for such growth pose a number of challenges.

First, as a consequence of this dependence, CLTB is obliged to follow strict policies and procedures required by governmental entities for certain aspects of CLTB's daily operation. Aspirations and value systems of CLTB and public institutions are not always similar, and strict governmental frameworks have an impact on CLTB's autonomy. For instance, when using public subsidies, CLTB is obliged to adopt public tendering procedures, complicating the participative nature of the development process.

Second, CLTB is particularly vulnerable to political changes (Aernouts, 2017); that is, every change in the regional government can lead to a new positioning of acceptance and support for the community land trust model. Every four years, CLTB has to win the trust of the political party in charge and enter into a new relationship. Strategic battles and power games between political parties add to the difficulty. In the beginning of 2017, for instance, a regime change within the regional government led to the party in power giving serious consideration to forcing the CLT Brussels to transfer ownership of its lands to other housing providers in Brussels. Fortunately, thanks to the efforts of a strong network of supporters, this proposal, which would have undermined the entire rationale and operation of CLTB, was not adopted. But it demonstrates CLTB's vulnerability to changes in the political wind.

Meanwhile, political support for the CLT model is growing. After the regional elections in May 2019, the new government, composed of social democrats, greens, and regionalists, presented its coalition agreement. It stated that all public housing operators should make greater use of long-term lease contracts and that the government should "increase its support for the projects developed by Community Land Trust Brussels" and recognize CLTB as a "regional land alliance," accompanied by a management agreement so that CLTB can become "a partner in urban renewal programs."

Thirdly, the increase in scale and professionalization adds a dose of bureaucratization to CLTB's operations, even as the organization strives to remain a community-led movement that is guided and governed by its members. Also, as the number of inhabited homes steadily increases, CLTB will have to find ways to help residents to be fully in charge of managing their housing projects, while keeping them involved in the wider CLT movement.

In order to cope with these challenges, CLTB has entered into several agreements and has developed measures to increase its autonomy. Until recently, for example, CLTB has mainly worked with large, publicly-sponsored housing organizations such as the Housing Fund in managing its construction projects, but CLTB has decided to be in charge of its own construction management in the future. Naturally, this will create a whole new set of financial and organizational issues. CLTB will now have to finance and to staff building operations itself. Within its organization, a building division will have to be organised. Also, the double position of simultaneously being a builder and a community organizer can be challenging, especially when problems occur during the building process.

Next, CLTB has recently made efforts to attract private donors and investors to finance its operations. In 2017, for the first time, the organization started a fundraising campaign. This led to a few important gifts by private charity foundations a year later. CLTB wants to expand this practice in the near future by creating a land cooperative. Such a cooperative would enable civil investors to invest their money in the acquisition of community land for affordable housing and spaces for social, cultural, and economic activities. Alongside the Public Utility Foundation, which purchases land through grants and donations, CLTB's cooperative would purchase land with its shareholders' investments. Such a cooperative would not only increase CLTB's capacity and autonomy; it would also enable CLTB to diversify its production — for instance, by integrating rental units into its projects and by helping social and cultural projects to gain access to affordable land.

Furthermore, CLTB has worked hard to expand and to strengthen the larger CLT movement within Brussels, across Belgium, and in neighboring countries. By disseminating the model more widely, CLTB hopes more individuals and organizations will become active defenders of the community land trust. Since the very beginning of CLTB, its initiators have been making the case for CLTs in the rest of Belgium and Europe. Several conferences have been organized in Brussels, where invited guests from the UK and the USA have presented their work. At these gatherings, the foundation for an informal network among European activists, practitioners, and academics interested in the CLT model was laid. Later on, CLTB staff and board members have been regularly presenting their work. They helped the CLT in Ghent to take its first steps toward becoming established. After visiting CLTB, a busload of city officials, politicians, and legal experts from Lille (France) were convinced to adopt the model as well. This precipitated the enactment in France of national legislation enabling the establishment of CLTs (*Organismes de Foncier Solidaire*, OFS) and led to the creation of the country's first CLT, initiated by the municipal government in Lille. CLTB has also taken the initiative in bringing together urban CLTs from the northwest of Europe by starting Sustainable Housing for Inclusive and Cohesive Cities (SHICC), a project aimed at promoting further dissemination of the CLT model throughout Europe.[22]

> CLTB has taken the initiative in promoting further dissemination of the CLT model throughout Europe.

IV. (IN)CONCLUSION

CLTB has succeeded in building a solid operation in a relatively short period of time. Several precipitating or sustaining factors allowed this to happen: the CLTB network, composed of community organizations, neighborhood groups and housing activists; a housing policy traditionally paying great attention to homeownership, providing a favorable regime for developing owner-occupied CLT homes; new public budgets for affordable housing; the lagging construction of social housing; and the regional government's willingness to invest in socially innovative alternatives in the housing market. Another prerequisite for CLTB's success was the basic mentality of CLTB's initiators, members, and leaders, which has hovered between lobbying for their core values while implementing them with a level of pragmatism.

First, expanding and maintaining a broad network of both associations and public bodies has been essential. The close collaboration with a professional social housing organization such as the Brussels Housing Fund and with local community organizations, for example, was very important for developing the first real estate operations and for shaping the CLT community. CLTB's commitment to disseminate the model and to support start-up groups elsewhere also contributed to its own success, when CLTs in other cities and countries began referring to Brussels as an example worth emulating.

Second, CLTB's initiators have negotiated firmly to ensure the autonomy of the organization and to have residents and civil society represented on the board of directors.

Third, the organization has been relying on step-by-step problem-solving. The feasibility study that formed the basis for founding the CLTB more or less described the organization that is starting to take shape today. To get there, numerous obstacles had to be overcome, while almost all CLT components had to be (re)invented and adapted to the Brussels legal and political context. Today, for instance, now that more and more homes are becoming occupied, much thought is being given to how CLTB can help residents to manage their condominiums.

Although CLTB has succeeded in operationalizing the CLT model in the Brussels Capital Region and in developing several successful housing projects, the organization is today facing significant challenges in going to scale. In the years ahead, CLTB will have to diversify its resources, attracting private investors and donors. It will have to strengthen its regional legislative framework to ensure continued regional support. It will have to create the internal capacity and expertise to fiscally optimize the construction of new projects. New competences within the organization, such as project development and condominium management support, will have to be developed. CLTB must also be diligent in protecting its autonomy despite its dependency on governmental funding, while preserving the predominant role of residents and civil society in governing the organization. The staff, board, and membership of CLTB will have to be steadfast in continuing to advocate for the central position of *community* within a community land trust.

> *Such advocacy does not aim to replace the social housing policy that already exists, but to supplement it.*

Beyond dealing with these many issues, CLTB hopes to work with its allies inside and outside of government to structurally embed some key CLT principles into the government's regular housing policy and spatial policy, including: non-speculative land use; permanent affordability of publicly subsidized homeownership; and community participation in the development of affordable housing and in the governance of the organizations doing development. Such advocacy does not aim to *replace* the social housing policy that already exists, but to *supplement* it, making the general housing policy in Brussels and in Belgium more equitable, inclusive, and sustainable. Ultimately, CLTB aims to dissiminate the principle that lies at the heart of a community land trust, the principle that elevates the use value of real estate over its exchange value.

Ten years ago, a community land trust in Brussels was still an utopian idea, a distant dream of a small number of activists and community workers. Today, Community Land Trust Brussels is firmly established. The organisation has removed from the Brussels real estate market the first small pieces of land, colouring in the first pieces of a map where other rules apply. There is still a lot of work to be done before this unique approach to integrating resident participation into the design and operation of permanently affordable housing on land that is community-owned becomes mainstream. But CLTB is ready and eager to accept the challenge.

Fig. 4.5. CLTB staff, 2018. ANTOINE MEYER

—

2021 POSTSCRIPT:
SURVIVING THE PANDEMIC, SUPPORTING OUR FAMILIES, SUSTAINING OUR WORK

Geert De Pauw

One of the highlights for CLTB in 2020 should have been a celebratory book launch for *On Common Ground* that was planned to happen during a major international community land trust conference in Brussels. But COVID came, and the events were cancelled. These were not the only casualties of the pandemic, of course, a crisis which affected the work of CLTB and the people served by CLTB, a crisis likely to have lasting effects on our projects and activities.

COVID starkly demonstrated the importance of decent, affordable housing — and how unevenly housing opportunities are distributed in Brussels. Low-income families in overcrowded and poorly equipped housing suffered badly from the pandemic lockdown. The renewed attention being paid by government to the importance of housing led to some new policy proposals and CLTB was recognized as being a good practice in some of them. Unfortunately, this has not yet translated into concrete changes in public policy.

COVID also led to renewed attention being paid to the importance of open space in the city. The pressure to preserve the last unbuilt spaces for recreation and nature is increasing. Some of these spaces are where CLTB had hoped to build future homes, however, so it is becoming more difficult to find affordably priced, buildable land. CLTB has started giving more thought, therefore, to how we can build in a more ecologically responsible way. Together with our Brussels and European partners, we have started thinking about the role that the CLT model can play in promoting what the English economist, Kate Raworth, has called the "donut economy."[23] We believe, in fact, that our community-led, non-speculative way of working can help to make balanced choices for the development of these sites in a responsible, sustainable way.

COVID caused some delays in the construction of CLTB's projects and construction costs skyrocketed because of commodity price increases. As a result, we had to somewhat adjust our ambitions with regard to the production of new homes. Nevertheless, our portfolio grew significantly during the past year. Residents moved into two projects, *le Nid* in Anderlecht (7 homes and a community space) and *Arc-en-Ciel* in Molenbeek (32 homes and a community centre for women). By the end of 2020, therefore, we had expanded our holdings to 49 homes. By the end of 2021, we plan to have added another 50 homes to CLTB's portfolio.

A major breakthrough of the past two years was the approval of a recognition procedure for CLTs by the Brussels government.[24] There is now a legal framework that defines what a CLT is and that sets out the conditions for receiving support from the Brussels

Region. This will consolidate CLTB's place in the Brussels housing landscape and will make it easier for us to plan for the long term. CLTB will now be able to benefit from a number of measures that apply to recognized housing actors, such as the discounted VAT rate of 6% for the construction of social housing.

The increase in CLTB's investment budget, from €2 million annually to €3 million, is another proof of the government's endorsement and support for our community land trust. This an important step toward becoming the "government partner" alluded to above in the title of the present chapter.

At CLTB, for quite some time, we have been reflecting on the possibility of creating a new organizational structure that would allow us to attract citizen and impact investments, beyond the funding we raise from government sources. Such private investments would not only help us to develop our projects; they would enable us to maintain our autonomy, to acquire more resources, and to diversify our activities. At the end of 2020, we set up Fair Ground Brussels, together with a range of partners. This social real estate cooperative, based on the CLT model, aims to create rental housing for the homeless and working spaces for the social economy, among other assets contributing to thriving communities.

Our current activities are not limited to real estate production, however. Working towards resilient communities remains an important objective for CLTB. Like many other associations, we had to put many of our community activities on hold because of the health and safety measures required as a response to COVID. Activities that brought people face-to-face all but stopped, but we continued to work on ways to support our residents in promoting community-building activities in and around their housing projects. We are taking the first steps toward developing our buildings into sustainable mobility hubs for the neighborhoods in which they are located, we are preparing homework support classes for CLTB children, and we are making plans with our residents to start community kitchens.

As more and more residents move into CLTB homes, we will need to prove that CLTB's approach to equitable and sustainable development extends beyond building permanently affordable housing. If we succeed in doing so, we will be able to grow bigger and to spread further. We will be able to make a deeper impact on the quality of life for people and places we serve and to make a lasting contribution toward solving social and racial inequalities that the COVID pandemic once again exposed.

Notes

1. After West London, Luxembourg, and Hamburg.

2. The so-called "At Risk of Poverty or Social Exclusion" (AROPE), an indicator developed in the framework of the Europe 2020 strategy, measures the share of people that meets at least one of the following conditions: 1) the household's disposable income is below the national poverty risk limit; 2) is between 0 and 59 years old and lives in a family with a very Low Work Intensity (LWI); 3) is in Severe Material Deprivation (SMD).

3. This means they have a foreign nationality, they are born with a foreign nationality, or one of their parents has a foreign nationality.

4. The term "poor crescent" refers to the crescent-shaped sequence of neighbourhoods marked by a concentration of poverty indicators.

5. In 1989, the federal government of Belgium delegated housing policy to the regions of Brussels, Flanders, and Wallonia. This has been part of a larger federalization process, in which different former federal state domains were transferred to the regions.

6. The Brussels Capital Region has only recently abolished the housing bonus, a tax reduction for homeowners. It has replaced this measure by registration fee reduction, whereby all registration fees are waived on the first 175,000 EUR of a real estate purchase (Art. 46bis of Brussels-Capital Region's Registration, Mortgage, and Clerk's Office Fees Code).

7. Cheap loans are offered by the Brussels Housing Fund, a subsidized organization that also develops rental and owner-occupied housing for households with a low and modest income.

8. Thanks to regional support, Citydev.brussels, a "regional development company," develops homes and sells them to middle-income households for only two-thirds of their market value. In addition, the buyer can buy the property with a reduced VAT rate of 6%.

9. This information is explicitly mentioned on the Citydev-website: *https://www.citydev. brussels/nl/onze-filosofie*.

10. Between 2001 and 2011, the proportion of homeowners in the BCR fell from 42.7% to 38.81% (CENSUS 2011).

11. The Belgians who participated in this study visit were Michel Renard, from the Municipality of Molenbeek, Loïc Géronnez from Periferia, Geert De Pauw from Community Centre Bonnevie, and Thomas Dawance, researcher. Geert and Thomas later became part of CLTB's first staff.

12. For more on this dynamic, see: *http://www.periferia.be/Bibliomedia/PUB/EP2011/ periferia_2011_construire_politique_publique.pdf.*

13. The Brussels Housing Code includes all instruments and measures of the housing policy in the Brussels Capital Region.

14. For several CLTB projects, the Brussels Housing Fund, a subsidized organization that also develops rental and owner-occupied housing for households with a low and modest income, has acted as the building's developer.

15. Each year, the European Union launches "Urban Innovative Actions," supporting the development of innovative and participative projects around Europe that address urban challenges. Urban authorities, together with key stakeholders such as agencies, associations, private sector organisations, research institutions and NGOs are eligible to submit proposals.

16. Interestingly, Louvain-la-Neuve will be one of the first Belgian cities, after Brussels and Ghent, to start a community land trust. After being elected in 2018, the new mayor launched a plan for building 140 CLT homes, as part of a bigger new sustainable neighbourhood.

17. In French, Association Sans But Lucratif (ASBL).

18. In French, Fondation d'Utilité Public, a non-profit entity different from an ASBL, mainly used for the management of assets. One of the important differences between them is that a Foundation doesn't have members, making it very difficult to implement the CLT governance principles. CLTB resolved this issue by determining that board members of the Foundation would be designated by the members of the ASBL.

19. The representatives of the first two groups are elected by the NGO's general assembly. The government representatives are designated by the government, and approved by the assembly. Members of the Foundation's board are designated by the members of the ASBL, thus guaranteeing a strong link between both entities.

20. For the first projects, these groups were composed at the moment CLTB purchased land, thus enabling the future residents to have a say in the content of the public tender for an architectural project. Because of the long process in building any project, this meant that groups were composed 5 to 6 years before the residents could move into their homes. Today, groups are composed later on in the process, once the building permit is obtained, reducing the preparation period for homeowners to 2 or 3 years, if all goes well.

21. The vast majority of potential buyers have a migrant background, with a predominance of people with roots in Guinea, Morocco, and Congo. Furthermore, most of the families have a very modest income or benefit from a replacement income.

22. SHICC is a three-year initiative funded by the European Union. CLT Brussels, CLT Ghent, the London CLT, and the Lille CLT are SHICC's founding members.

23. "Doughnut economics" is a visual framework for sustainable development — shaped like a doughnut — combining the concept of ecological boundaries with the complementary concept of social boundaries, balancing the needs of the planet with the needs of people. See: Kate Raworth, *Donut Economics: Seven Ways to Think Like a 21st Century Economist.* London: Penguin Random House, UK, 2017.

24. Arrêté du Gouvernement de la Région de Bruxelles-Capitale organisant les Alliances foncières régionales, leur agrément et leur financement, 01/04/2021

References

Aernouts, N. and Ryckewaert, M. (2017). "Beyond housing: On the role of commoning in the establishment of a Community Land Trust project," *International Journal of Housing Policy* 18 (4), 503–521.

Aernouts, N., Ryckewaert, M. van Heur, B., and Moritz, B. (2017). *Housing the social. Investigating the role of commoning in the development of social housing initiatives.* Unpublished doctoral thesis.

De Pauw, G. (2011). *Passieve woningen, actieve bewoners* (Brussels: Opbouwwerk).

Dessouroux, C., Bensliman, R., Bernard, N., De Laet, S., Demonty, F., Marissal, P. and Surkyn, J. (2016). "Huisvesting in Brussel: diagnose en uitdagingen," *Brussels Studies* 99, 1–32.

Englert, M., Luyten, S., Fele, D., Mazina, D., Mendes Da Costa, E. and Missinne, S. for Commission Communautaire Commune (2018). *Welzijnsbarometer 2018.* Brussels: Observatoire de la santé et du social.

Geurts, V. and Goossens, L. (2004). "Home ownership and social inequality in Belgium." (In K. Kurz and H.P. Blossfeld. *Home Ownership and Social Inequality in Comparative Perspective,* Stanford, California: Stanford University Press, 79–113.

Loopmans, M. and Kesteloot, C. (2009). "Social inequalities." *Brussels Studies* 16, 1–12.

Romainville, A. (2010). "Who benefits from home ownership support?" *Brussels Studies* 34, 1–20.

Vermeulen, S. (2009). *Needed: an intelligent and integrated vision for Brussels' urban planning.* Paper presented at the 4th International Conference of the International Forum on Urbanism (IFoU), Amsterdam/Delft.

5.

Beyond England
Origins and Evolution of the Community Land Trust Movement in Europe

Geert De Pauw and Joaquin de Santos

This chapter traces the context in which the European community land trust (CLT) movement was born and evolved, both from a broader European perspective and within individual countries. The scope of this chapter is to look at developments outside of England, mostly on the mainland of Europe, but recent developments in Scotland and Ireland are included as well. We take stock of the current state of the movement, highlighting similarities and differences in the ways that CLTs are structured and applied in different countries, and look ahead to the future prospects for CLT development. We also trace important connections that are being forged between CLTs in Europe and CLTs in England through a cross-national project known as "Sustainable Housing for Inclusive and Cohesive Cities."

We will first look at the broader context of housing production in Europe. As in other geographies, the production of housing in Western Europe has undergone significant changes over the last forty years. In the post-Second World War period, public authorities took the initiative in developing large numbers of housing units to accomodate those affected by the War but also to tackle the remaining pockets of inadequate housing in cities. This often led to massive housing developments that were often built at great speed and with lower-quality materials in formerly rural areas at the periphery of major cities.

In parallel, the evolution of the global economy towards more office-based jobs has created the impetus to build large office buildings in central areas (sometimes at the expense of historical neighbourhoods) or in areas with good transport links, restructuring urban space to give way to the automobile. The lucrative market in office estate has resulted in collusion between real estate developers and local politicians in many cities.

Another major development of this post-war period has been the increased earnings by a large portion of the working population as a result of the economic boom.

Lower-middle-class households could now afford to buy residential property, which was being delivered on a massive scale by real estate developers. Public policies were introduced to subsidize homeownership. As a result, these populations increasingly deserted public housing.

This post-war paradigm, often dubbed "Fordist" in relation to the logic of increasing the purchasing power of workers to enable them to acquire Ford automobiles, has given way since the 1980s to a model where the market takes on a more important role in the provision of housing. This shift has been accompanied, in many cases, by a virtual stagnation of the production of public housing (with the notable exception of France, the Netherlands, some Scandinavian countries, along with a few major cities, such as Vienna).

The evolution of the global economy during this period has created significant imbalances, with an increasing concentration of economic development in larger cities and, at times, an abrupt economic decline of former industrial areas that once had substantial manufacturing capacities. This has fostered greater competition between cities to capture capital flows that are increasingly global and volatile, caused in part by the deregulation of financial markets since the mid-1980s. One outcome is that housing in many European cities has become increasingly expensive and commodified.

These trends were accelerated by the global financial crisis starting in 2008. While housing markets in many European countries slumped as a result of the drought of real estate financing, the massive public injections of capital into failing banks quickly became a financial force of their own. Investors began looking for returns in markets that had been less financialised and profitable in the past, but were now looking like good investment opportunities. The housing market was the most important of those untapped markets, offering attractive returns that could sometimes reach double digits. As a consequence, massive amounts of capital were injected into housing, driving up prices not only in the most desirable locations, but also in neighbourhoods across entire urban areas.

In a number of areas, long-term residents were starting to get priced out of their neighbourhoods. Households had to dedicate an ever-greater share of their incomes for housing in many European countries, with even more acute situations arising in many major European cities. In other urban neighbourhoods, economic decline and a lack of investment caused an accelerated degradation of the housing stock.

With governments in many countries struggling to provide effective policy responses to these mounting problems, CLTs were envisaged and implemented as a possible solution to the affordable housing crisis. Local communities in England had begun adopting, in the early 2000s, a version of the CLT model that had been pioneered in the United States, adapting it to their own circumstances. In Brussels, local non-profits created the first continental European CLT in 2012. Municipal governments started considering the CLT model as a suitable policy response in countries such as France in 2014. Interest in the model has now spread to several other European countries.

EMERGENCE OF A CLT MOVEMENT IN MAINLAND EUROPE

In 2009, a group of community organizers and activists for the right to housing in Brussels started looking for a community-led strategy for producing permanently affordable housing. They first thought of the cooperative model. Cooperative housing organisations, often originating in the labour movement, had initiated many interesting projects in Belgium. For example, many of the garden neighbourhoods from the interwar period, inspired by Ebenezer Howard's Garden Cities, had a clear emancipatory and utopian character and were progressive in terms of urban planning and architecture. However, by the beginning of the Twenty-First Century, many of these cooperative societies had lost much of their original dynamism. Many of them, moreover, had been absorbed into a regional social housing system. Within this rigid framework, it was almost impossible to develop innovative projects; nor was it possible to create new cooperative social housing companies.

Those activists who became the initiators of the Brussels CLT (CLTB) explored the possibility of establishing a cooperative society outside the framework of social housing. That was not so easy, because this legal form was unsuitable for housing projects in Belgium. During their search for a solution, they read about an international colloquium on new forms of cooperative living in Lyon. There, they heard Professor Yves Cabannes talk about CLTs, and understood that this could be what they were looking for. Soon thereafter, in 2009, some of them had the opportunity to take part in an international study visit to the Champlain Housing Trust, which had just won the UN World Habitat Award. The trip to Burlington lit the spark. The people from Brussels met not only CLT pioneers from Vermont, but also people who were trying to get CLTs off the ground in England and Australia. The Brussels CLT was started within an international environment, therefore, and has continued to nourish that global dimension ever since.

CLTB played a major, precipitating role in helping the model to spread in Belgium and across the entire European mainland. The success of the CLT in Brussels, along with the examples of the London CLT, the Champlain Housing Trust, and the Dudley Street Neighbourhood Initiative in Boston, inspired the people who are now working in various European cities to establish their own CLTs. A number of key figures from the National CLT Network in the United States actively supported these European and English developments. They made information available, gave long-distance advice, and came to Europe several times to explain the model, talk about its origins, and testify about American CLTs. An important step was taken in 2013. The Platform CLT Ghent, CLT Brussels and the ACW, the Christian trade union movement, organized a two-day conference about CLTs in Belgium and Europe. Brenda Torpy and Tony Pickett from the United States and Dave Smith from the London CLT came to talk about their experiences, addressing an audience that consisted not only of Belgians but also of people from across Europe. In 2014, another CLT advocate from the USA, John Davis, paid visits to Flanders, Wallonia, and Brussels, giving a dozen talks over a four-day period. Here, too, there were people in attendance from outside the Belgian borders.

The American CLT Network also invited Europeans to their own conferences to report on their progress. European and global networks and organizations such as World Habitat, Housing Europe, Feantsa, and the Cohabitat Network also played a role in disseminating the model. Interest from the academic world began gradually to increase as well. In 2017, the European Union funded the SHICC project (see below), which helped to consolidate this energy and to lay the foundation for structured cooperation across European borders.

> They placed an emphasis on using rather than possessing, on common property rather than individual property.

Through all of these conferences, presentations, and meetings, it became clear that interest in this innovative model was great. CLTs seemed to be not only a way of tackling the worsening housing problems being experienced by many European cities, but also a way of responding to the economic crisis of 2008. The absence of effective responses and innovative thinking from the public sector convinced many private citizens it was time to develop alternative models themselves. The concept of "the Commons" regained interest as an alternative economic model. Everywhere in European cities, citizens began to experiment with energy cooperatives, local currencies, community gardens, food teams, tool libraries, community supported agriculture, and cooperative supermarkets, initiatives that were being developed alongside the market. They placed an emphasis on using rather than possessing, on common property rather than individual property. They attempted to deal cautiously with the limited resources that the planet offers us, rather than assuming unbridled growth. They promoted greater solidarity in place of rising inequalities. Although some of these initiatives relied on support from the state, they developed mostly in the spaces between the market and the state, attaching greater importance to civil society and self-government. Many activists and advocates for the Commons, in particular, saw in the CLT another way to apply principles of the Commons to the production and management of homes and neighbourhoods. Within this ferment of activity and experimentation, the rather unusual model of the community land trust was recognized as something compatible with their values and was seized upon by citizens in search of new alternatives.

CLT DEVELOPMENTS IN SELECTED COUNTRIES

Belgium

In Belgium, residents in Ghent were the first to show curiosity about the CLT initiative unfolding in Brussels. In April 2010, the community organisation *Samenlevingsopbouw*

Gent stirred up interest in the CLT model among a number of partners and organized a train trip to Brussels. There, they visited the housing project *L'Espoir* in Molenbeek and met with initiators of the Brussels CLT, which was still being established. In January 2012, these visitors finished a feasibility study for creating a new CLT in Ghent. A month later, they brought together a steering group composed of civil society organizations and experts, who were later joined by future residents. In March 2012, twenty-seven civil society organizations and government officials signed the *CLT Ghent Charter*. In September of that same year, they presented the results of the feasibility study at a seminar, which included lectures by Dave Smith from the London CLT and Geert De Pauw from Platform CLT Brussels. In 2013, CLT Gent and CLT Brussels, together with ACW, published *Stapstenen tussen Koop en Huur* ("Stepping Stones between Buying and Renting"). This brochure has since been used to increase the knowledge about community land trusts in Flanders, among everyone involved in the social housing field. Thanks to the CLT initiative in Ghent, political parties started to refer to CLTs in their programs, and Flemish experts and academics started to write about the model.

After a quick start, however, it took a while before CLT Ghent could put their ideas into practice. In contrast to the Brussels Region, the Flemish regional government did not give the CLT in Ghent the financial support it needed to purchase land for the development of affordable housing.

Today, CLT Ghent operates on two tracks. Through the program *Dampoort KnapT OP*, the CLT helps owner-occupiers renovate their properties via a rolling fund. Resale of renovated properties is controlled in accordance with the CLT's anti-speculative formula. In 2015, the first ten renovated homes were completed, and the project is now being continued thanks to funding from the European Union.

In the district of Meulestede, CLT Ghent now wants to develop a housing project with thirty-four homes, a 1,500-square-meter community garden, and a community space. The first plans for this development date back to 2013. As of 2020, construction is being prepared. The City of Ghent, owner of the land, has agreed upon a long-term lease on the land. A social housing company, WoninGent, will build the homes. Currently, partners are in the process of choosing an architect. If everything goes well, the first stone can be laid in 2020 and, by 2022, the first residents will move into their new CLT homes.

Ghent also took the initiative of establishing the Flemish CLT coalition, composed of some fifteen civil society organizations. This platform continued and extended CLT Ghent's efforts in propagating the model. The platform's efforts have contributed to the exploration of the CLT model in other Flemish cities.

In Leuven, a city that has faced rising house prices in recent last years, the city commissioned CLT Brussels and the research group Cosmopolis to carry out a feasibility study in 2019, with the intention of setting up a CLT in this university city in 2020. In Bruges, too, local public actors have expressed the wish to start a CLT. In Antwerp, the municipality and civil society organizations are exploring the possibility of redeveloping part of an old hospital site into CLT housing. In other Belgian cities, such as Ostend, social housing companies are examining the possibility of adopting the model.

In 2012, a CLT coalition was set up in the Walloon Region, as was previously the case in Brussels and Flanders. This coalition started lobbying for the regional government to make resources available to enable the development of CLTs. In 2014, the Walloon Minister of Housing launched the *Construire du Logement pour Tous* programme (the attentive reader will recognize the resulting acronym), which would give municipal governments and local housing organisations the opportunity to start a CLT. This attracted a great deal of attention from municipalities, but when it turned out that the funding made available by the regional government was going to be insufficient to acquire land, most municipalities lost interest.

The Walloon coalition then tried to develop a pilot project itself. They wanted to convert an empty monastery into a mixed-use project with affordable housing and a social economy project combining food production and a restaurant. They succeeded in persuading the owners to leave them the property, if they could prove the feasibility of the project. They are still raising the funds for the needed renovation, so the project is temporarily on hold. At the same time, a number of Walloon municipalities have taken a renewed interest in creating

> CLTs in Belgium are similar to what is sometimes called the "classic" CLT in the United States.

CLTs. For example, the new mayor of Ottignies/Louvain-la-Neuve has made it a policy priority, and in Comines-Warneton the municipal authorities are in the process of facilitating the establishment of CLTs.

Others in Belgium have also begun working with CLT ideas. Cohousing groups see in the legal model that the Brussels CLT has invented an alternative to the co-ownership model or the cooperative model, neither of which has fully met their expectations. Instead, by using a public interest foundation as the landowner, and by giving long-term leases to the homeowners, cohousing groups can now limit resale prices, they can control who will be the new buyers, and they have an organizational model that makes it possible to govern their projects in a democratic way. The Fondus des Petits Marais, for example, in the vicinity of Mons, has adopted features of the CLT model in its operation.

Among the many CLTs being started or planned in Belgium, there is some variation in the way they are handling the ownership of real estate and the way they are structuring the membership and governance of the CLT itself. Nevertheless, up to now, CLTs in Belgium have been organized generally along lines that are similar to what is sometimes called the "classic" CLT in the United States. Thus, the land is owned by one party and the building is owned by another. The CLT has a voting membership that elects a majority of the seats on the governing board. That board is divided into three parts, representing current and future owners, civil society, and local government. The housing that is built on the CLT's land is made permanently affordable via provisions contained in the ground lease.

Development of the Organismes de Foncier Solidaire in France
Authored by Audrey Linkenheld[1]

Activists from the academic and non-profit sectosr have been promoting the community land trust model in France for a number of years, leading to the enactment in 2014 of national legislation defining and authorizing the French version of the CLT and creating a new form of long-term ground lease. Local governments, public land organisations, and cooperative social housing organisations are currently taking the lead in implementing a national network, *Organismes de Foncier Solidaire,* throughout France. The City of Lille has played a pioneering role in laying the foundation for this fledgling—and uniquely French—CLT movement.

Lille is a prime example of a French city that was affordable until the early 2000s, but then experienced increasing pressure on its housing market as a result of high demand from students and from small households who found employment in the metropolitan area. Meanwhile, turnover in the city's social housing slowed down because poorer families were finding it increasingly difficult to move into housing in the open market as a result of the sudden rise in housing prices.

In 2008, the City of Lille adopted a comprehensive housing policy aimed at doubling the number of new housing units developed within the city, while requiring a set-aside of up to 45% of affordable housing (rental or sales) in all new residential developments of more than seventeen units. This policy supported the development of more than 3000 affordably priced units sold to households under a specific income threshold defined by the City.

The challenge that arose, however, was how to preserve this supply of affordable housing, which had been made possible by massive financial support from the municipality. The City of Lille had imposed anti-speculative clauses, but they proved insufficient in protecting the affordability of these heavily subsidized homes. This is why, as a Member of Parliament, and inspired by the example of CLTs in the USA and Belgium, I championed national legislation to enable the creation of a new type of non-profit organization, *Organismes de Foncier Solidaire (OFS),* the French version of a CLT.[2]

After this legislation was enacted in March 2014, the next step was to create a new type of long-term ground lease, the *bail réel solidaire (BRS).* This lease, lasting 19 to 99 years, allows land to be permanently owned by an OFS and, because it permits the ownership of land and buildings to be separated, it makes housing more affordable, since households do not have to pay for the underlying land. Clauses in the BRS also impose a limit on future prices when homes are resold. This safeguards for generations to come the public subsidies that were used to buy the land and to reduce the purchase price of the housing.

The first OFS was born in Lille in February 2017. Fifteen permanently affordable homes using a BRS lease have already been built and successfully marketed. They are part of a mixed-income, mixed-use project in an attractive neighbourhood in the city centre that will include 210 housing units (open market and social), a hotel, offices for non-profits, and an art gallery. The buyers of these fifteen homes on leased land benefited from a

> The challenge was how to preserve this affordable housing, made possible by financial support from the municipality.

very affordable price of 2110€/sqm instead of 5300€/sqm, which is what they would have had to pay without the OFS. A second OFS project with seventeen units, offered for sale at the same price, will soon be developed in the same area.[3]

Many other cities, including Rennes, Nantes, and Paris, have begun creating OFSs of their own. Meanwhile, the French Federation of Social Housing Cooperatives has encouraged the formation of OFSs by local cooperatives in places as diverse as Saint-Malo, the Basque Country, and the regions of Provence-Alpes-Côte d'Azur and Rhone-Alpes. Public landowning organisations (*Etablissements Publics Fonciers Locaux*) are also exploring the creation of OFSs in Haute Savoie, in the Basque Country, in Franche Comté, and in the overseas territories of French Guyana and la Réunion.

To date, nineteen OFSs have been established, with plans to produce 1000 permanently affordable, owner-occupied homes within the next two to three years. In 2018, following a proposal put forward by Lille, they joined together to form a new national network of OFSs, *Foncier Solidaire—France*.[4]

Netherlands[5]

Major Dutch cities such as Rotterdam and Amsterdam have been confronted with housing problems similar to those in other European cities. In Amsterdam, for example, the average sales price for housing quadrupled between 1995 and 2017. The pressure on the housing market also increased as non-profit housing corporations became less able to address the problems of pricing and supply. The Netherlands is a country with a large stock of social housing that is rented out to people with low and modest incomes. These homes have been mainly developed and managed by large housing corporations. The position of the housing corporations has been weakened, however, by decreasing governmental support, mismanagement and scandals at some of the housing corporations, and increasing pressure from the European Commission to reduce "state aid," regarded as a cause of market distortion. The housing corporations have been building less affordable housing than in the past and many of the corporations' homes have been sold to private investors on the market. Despite the Netherlands' well-deserved reputation as a country with a large stock of social housing, the waiting time for social housing in some urban neighbourhoods is now more than ten years.

It is no coincidence, therefore, that the first two initiatives to consider applying the community land trust model in the Netherlands have had a link with a social housing corporation.

In Rotterdam, the urban activists of *Stad in de Maak* (City in the Making) have concluded an agreement with the Havensteder Corporation to refurbish vacant buildings and to use them temporarily for three to ten years. These buildings are managed partly as commons: the rooms are rented, mainly to young people. On the ground floor, there is room for all kinds of social and productive activities, such as a neighbourhood canteen, a micro cinema, a launderette, and a woodcraft workshop. *City in the Making* is now reflecting on ways of getting these buildings, as well as others, off the market for good. In order to achieve this, they are exploring different strategies. They are involved in Vrijcoop, the Dutch version of the German *Mietshäuser Syndikat* model of rental housing cooperatives. This association pursues very similar goals as a community land trust, although the approach is somewhat different. Vrijcoop guarantees the continued affordability of solidarity housing projects, spread across the Netherlands, by taking shares in the projects. In parallel, members of City in the Making are also examining possibilities for the CLT model to serve as a supplement or replacement for the leasehold (*erfpacht*) model that is widely used in the Netherlands.[6]

In Amsterdam, two companies active in the social innovation sector, *And the People* and *Publieke Versnellers,* jointly took the initiative in 2018 to explore the potential of the CLT model through design thinking. As a part of their analyses, these companies looked for a suitable neighbourhood to carry out action research. They ended up in the Bijlmer, a huge modernist social high-rise district constructed in the 1960s and 1970s in Amsterdam Southeast. They soon made contact with the Maranatha Community, a religious community mainly from the African diaspora which organizes community-building and emancipatory activities in this neighbourhood.

In August 2018, these stakeholders organized a three-day design workshop in the Bijlmer where representatives from the housing corporation, the City of Amsterdam, local residents, interested social investors and all sorts of experts came together to think about the concept of possibly creating a CLT. They then organized a series of workshops in the neighbourhood. In December, a busload of Amsterdammers made the journey to Brussels to take part in a peer-to-peer exchange in the context of the European SHICC project (see below). They have now set up a steering group and have begun making contact with policymakers and interested investors. Their intention is to create dwellings and community infrastructure in the Bijlmer through new construction or the renovation of existing buildings, within the general framework of a CLT.

Germany[7]

In Germany, the Trias Foundation and the Switzerland-based Edith Maryon Foundation have been using long-term lease contracts to ensure the permanent affordability of community-led housing, productive spaces, and community facilities for decades. Both organizations own a few hundred parcels of land on which local communities have developed all kinds of projects, including Ex-Rotaprint in Berlin, a former industrial site which is now providing spaces for artists and other "makers" in the service of *Arbeit, Kunst, Soziales* (Work, Art, Community).[8] The Trias Foundation and the Edith Maryon Foundation share the same philosophy as CLTs, with regard to the long-term stewardship of land. They are not themselves CLTs, however. Their service areas cover all of Germany in the case of the Trias Foundation, and both Germany and Switzerland in the case of the Maryon Foundation. Residents who occupy the permanently affordable housing and non-residential buildings on lands that are leased from these foundations are not represented on the governing board of either foundation.

The first real CLT initiative in Germany is currently emerging in Berlin. Inspired by CLT success stories in the USA and by more recent examples of successful CLTs in Brussels and London, an informal CLT planning group was organized at the end of 2017 in the Berlin District of Friedrichshain-Kreuzberg. Housing experts, community activists, researchers, project developers, and representatives of local government have been meeting together. This CLT initiative is a response to a mounting crisis caused by exploding land values, soaring rents, and diminishing access to housing.

> The land beneath these buildings would be permanently removed from the market and managed by the new CLT-inspired organisation.

Supported by the District's Councillor for Planning and Building, who provided funding for an initial feasibility study, this CLT initiative is building on decades of activism and community-led development in the district's neighbourhoods. Strong activist traditions include squatting and many forms of self-help, self-organized and cooperative housing, as well as collective and non-profit practices for coordinating everything from small-scale industry to community gardening. The current plan is to create a new local and democratic organisation in 2020, based on the CLT model. The organisation's goal is to make a significant contribution to Berlin's housing movement by promoting private, non-speculative forms of common ownership and project development, as a complement to existing models of cooperative housing.

Initial projects are likely to involve rescuing existing older buildings in partnership with their current residents. The land beneath these buildings would be permanently removed from the market and managed by the new CLT-inspired organisation. A housing cooperative would assume ownership of the buildings and management of combinations of residential and commercial spaces, with a long-term lease for the underlying land. Provisions in the ground lease would define future uses of the land and buildings, as well as the ongoing relationship between the owner of the land (that is, the CLT organisation) and owners of the buildings. Financing and subsidies are expected to be forthcoming from public sources, as well as from private institutions and individuals. Future projects may include the provision of social spaces, commercial spaces, and community gardens, as well as the construction of new buildings.

Italy[9]

The CLT model was introduced to Italy by Homers, a non-profit organisation that is dedicated to developing community-led affordable housing. After meeting people from CLTs in Belgium and England, Homers convened a roundtable discussion of the CLT concept in Turin in 2014 to which CLT practitioners from other countries were invited.[10]

The meeting just happened to coincide with the occupation of the old royal stables, *Cavallerizza Reale,* a huge vacant historic space in Turin's city centre. CLT advocates met with the occupiers of *Cavallerizza* and discussed the possibility of applying the CLT concept to redevelopment of the royal stables. Although that particular project was never realized, the discussions around it did eventually lead to some interest in the model from the Chieri municipality, near Turin.

Starting in 2010, Chieri had joined with a few other Italian cities to develop "commons regulations," a regulatory framework outlining how local governments, citizens, and the local community can manage public and private spaces and assets together. Chieri became the first municipality to integrate the CLT model into its commons regulations as one option for common management. The City of Palermo later did the same. The idea in both cities was that the municipality would transfer empty buildings or underused plots of land to a community land trust.

In Chieri, Homers negotiated with the city government for the acquisition of two sites, *Tabasso* and *Cascina Maddalene.* Detailed legal and financial plans for the redevelopment of these derelict sites as community land trusts were made, but in the end the municipality wasn't ready to collaborate, mainly because city officials worried whether the separation of land and buildings and the restriction on resale prices were "legal," despite being assured by a registered notary that they were. Despite this setback in Chieri, which may be temporary, Homers began working to develop another CLT project on a plot of church-owned land in Turin. This project will produce forty-two family flats and two shared flats of "supportive serviced housing" for families with a physically or mentally handicapped member. The complex will include community spaces, a public garden, a day care centre, a solidarity restaurant, a shop for local food produced by social co-ops, and healthcare facilities.

Switzerland[11]

Switzerland has a strong tradition of cooperative housing. At the beginning of the Twentieth Century, a number of cooperatives were set up to produce affordable housing for the working class. In the 1990s, this movement gained new dynamism. In the wake of a squatters' movement, new community-led cooperatives emerged, especially in cities such as Zurich, Lausanne, and Geneva. Thanks to the support of the respective urban authorities, these cooperatives have been able to expand considerably in recent years and have started to develop ever larger and more ambitious projects.

In Geneva, town planning rules determine the type of housing that can be built. Some building sites are reserved for cooperatives, but only rental housing can be built there because in Switzerland the classic housing cooperative is a *tenant* cooperative. The cooperative is the owner (or leaseholder) of the land and building. Members rent their housing units from the cooperative. Until recently, cooperatives have developed and managed only rental housing, so any land that became available for the construction of owner-occupied housing was *de facto* reserved for private for-profit developers.

CODHA, a large housing cooperative in Geneva, decided in 2018 to expand its activities to include owner-occupied homes developed through long-term lease contracts on land owned by a cooperative, homes that will remain permanently affordable through resale mechanisms. As in all its other projects, the residents will participate in the development and management of the homes. In this way, CODHA wants to respond to the wish of some members to become homeowners. By doing so, CODHA can also expand its activities beyond the areas that the city has reserved for tenant cooperatives.

The first homes in Switzerland that are being owned and operated in the manner of a CLT are being created under the auspices of a cooperative housing association that was founded in 1994, one which has long shared the same commitment to community-led development of permanently affordable housing that is found among CLTs in other countries. From now on, for part of its activities, CODHA will use the CLT ownership model. The *propriété sans but lucratif* (non-profit ownership housing), as they christened this branch of their work, will start its first developments in 2020.

Spain and Portugal[12]

The CLT model has gained a growing audience among scholars and NGOs in both Portugal and Spain. Although no CLTs yet exist in the Iberian Peninsula, the CLT model has been presented and discussed over the last few years in a number of venues and contexts, thanks mainly to the tireless efforts of Yves Cabannes and Antonio Manuel Rodríguez Ramos. It has attracted particular interest among neighbourhoods with semi-formal or informal land regimes, such as Cova da Moura in the metropolitan area of Lisbon.

The grassroots platform *Morar em Lisboa* (To Live in Lisbon) has shown an interest in the CLT model as a possible strategy for addressing the negative impact of extensive touristification on the people living in downtown Lisbon. There is also growing interest in the CLT model in Cañada Real, an informal settlement in Madrid where no titling solution has yet been found.

A major development of late has been the effort to remove legal hurdles to establishing a CLT in Spain. This initiative was carried out with students from the *Laboratorio Jurídico sobre Desahucios* (Legal Lab on Evictions), as a follow-up to the first session of the International Tribunal on Forced Evictions, organized by Rodríguez Ramos and Cabannes. A new legal framework for CLTs was developed by a group of trained legal professionals and has now been presented to the Andalusian Assembly.

Some municipal governments have recently taken note of the CLT as well. The City of Barcelona has undertaken a partnership with New York City under the International Urban Cooperation Programme of the European Union to work on affordable housing—with a particular focus on CLTs. Barcelona has also witnessed the development of *La Borda,* a housing cooperative that, while not being a CLT per se, shares many of its principles, including the separate ownership of the land and buildings, community involvement, and the inclusion of anti-speculative mechanisms designed to keep the housing permanently affordable. The first housing project of *La Borda* was inaugurated in 2018 with twenty-eight apartments.

Central and Eastern Europe

The situation in Central and Eastern Europe is unique compared to the rest of Europe. In the last 30 years, ever since the fall of the Berlin Wall, housing policy in these states has gone through a series of major changes. Policy was characterized by rapid privatization of state-owned housing after 1989. The real estate market then went through intensive growth between 2000 and 2008, followed by the collapse or stagnation of housing prices after the global financial crisis in 2008.

> They are responding to the housing emergency by taking the lead in reinventing types and tenures of housing from the bottom up.

Today, housing is left almost entirely to the market. Many households have neither the necessary capital to acquire an apartment nor to qualify for a mortgage. Households struggle to cover basic housing expenses. Many people are unable to afford their own apartment. Particularly for young people, this leads to an unhealthy dependence on older generations, increasing the pressures that cause many to leave the country. Also, the communist heritage gave community housing, cooperatives, and state housing, which were the standard forms of tenure in these countries for ages, a bad reputation. Nevertheless, across the region new cooperative housing developments are now being explored by pioneering groups. They are responding to the housing emergency—unaffordability, speculation, a negligible amount of social housing—by taking the lead in reinventing types and tenures of housing from the bottom up.

The MOBA Housing network is playing a leading role in fostering this reinvention. It gathers together grassroots practitioners who are working on housing initiatives in Zagreb, Budapest, Belgrade, Prague, and Ljubljana, looking for ways to build affordably priced, community-led housing. Today, all of these groups are looking into different organisational forms and financing possibilities. Cooperative housing has received the most attention to date, but in 2018 MOBA organised a meeting in Croatia to explore whether the CLT model might also have a place in addressing the housing problems of Central and Eastern Europe.

Scotland[13]

Scotland has the most concentrated pattern of landownership in the developed world. Over 80% of Scotland is in private ownership; and half of that private land is in the hands of fewer than 500 owners. The community land movement has been one response to this unequal distribution of ownership. In the 1990s, communities in the Highlands of Scotland were experiencing depopulation and decline, partly as a result of an inability to influence the way that the land where they lived was managed and developed. In response, several communities raised funds to purchase land and to shape their futures by ensuring their land was managed and developed in ways that provide collective community benefits through enhanced security of housing tenure, improved employment prospects, and sustainable land management.

> Around 230,000 hectares of Scotland are now in community ownership.

These early community landowners were able to turn around years of depopulation and decline through an ambitious approach to regeneration. They inspired others and provided a template for the subsequent purchase and development of land by communities, both rural and urban over the following decades. Now, around 230,000 hectares of Scotland are in community ownership. Democratically elected community trusts own the land on behalf of the communities that live there and are accountable to them for the management and development of the land. Communities have developed a huge range of assets and services on their land including renewables projects, affordable housing, business units, harbours and pontoons, and tourist facilities.

The Scottish Government established the Scottish Land Fund in 2001 to support the purchase of land by communities and, in 2003, Parliament established preemptive legal rights for communities to buy private land and buildings in certain circumstances.[14] In 2015, legislation provided a framework for the transfer of public assets to community organisations as well.[15] In 2016, the powers afforded to rural communities became applicable to urban Scotland. To exercise these Rights to Buy, communities need to have an appropriate governance structure (usually a company limited by guarantee) and must have demonstrated support for community ownership via a local ballot. The process of land reform is ongoing. In 2020, further legislation will be introduced to help communities buy land in pursuance of sustainable development.[16]

Community Land Scotland is the national network for community landowners and communities that are in the process of acquiring land. Historically, most community landowners were in rural areas, but Community Land Scotland is now also supporting a growing network of urban community landowners.

One significant example of an endeavour to apply all facets of Scottish community ownership to an urban setting is the Midsteeple Quarter project in Dumfries. This project intends to bring about mixed-use regeneration via a process of community ownership, incrementally acquiring all properties within an urban quarter and redeveloping them according to a masterplan for community facilities, business space and housing. The community organization behind this project was born out of many years of engagement, seeking to address the modern role of a market town within the context of town centre decline and absentee ownership. The group has acquired its first property within the Quarter and is taking its first steps toward delivery.

Ireland[17]

House prices in Ireland have risen enormously in recent years. Cities like Dublin have become unaffordable for many. Unlike in the UK, however, and despite the work over the past decade by people such as Emer O'Siochru and groups like the Community Land Trust Initiative, community land trusts have yet to become firmly established in Ireland.

In 2010, the *Manifesto for Rural Development* was published by the Carnegie UK Trust in association with a number of Irish actors, proposing the CLT as a vehicle for sustainable rural regeneration. Inspired by this publication, the Irish Regenerative Land Trust is currently developing a rural CLT.

The founding of the Land Development Agency (LDA) in 2018 was intended to streamline the provision of state and private land for affordable housing. The LDA and a number of local authorities have declared their intention of developing policies to enable CLTs. Limerick City, for example, is actively seeking to enable inner-city regeneration using the community land trust model.

There is limited understanding of the model in Ireland, however, and there has been neither recognition nor sanction by risk-averse state bodies. Private and religious institutions may offer a realistic alternative to the state as possible sources of land for CLTs. It is anticipated that Ireland will see the introduction of pilot CLTs in the main urban areas in the near future, and possibly in rural areas as well.

A EUROPEAN COLLABORATION TO ADVANCE CLTs: SUSTAINABLE HOUSING FOR INCLUSIVE AND COHESIVE CITIES (SHICC)

The leaders of the first urban CLTs in Europe and England turned to the European Union in search of financial resources for strengthening their fledgling movement. The European Union is not allowed to legislate with regard to housing, but social innovation is an increasingly popular policy area. Representatives of the London CLT and CLT Brussels, who had met in 2012 during a conference of the National CLT Network in the USA, partnered that year to apply for funding under an EU project call on innovation. They were not successful, but after two later attempts the European Union finally approved their proposal for a collaboration among urban CLTs in Belgium, England, and France. This project was given the name of "Sustainable Housing for Inclusive and Cohesive Cities" (SHICC). CLT Brussels took the initiative of forming the partnership, bringing together the leaders of various organizations who had met in recent years at conferences in the United States or in Europe.

Since its onset in 2017, the SHICC project has been able to achieve significant progress in four respects. First, it has played a major role as a catalyst of the European CLT movement, increasing its support base through meetings and events. The project's partners organised a major policy conference in May 2018 in Lille with speakers from a number of different countries and organisations. Around 150 participants from across

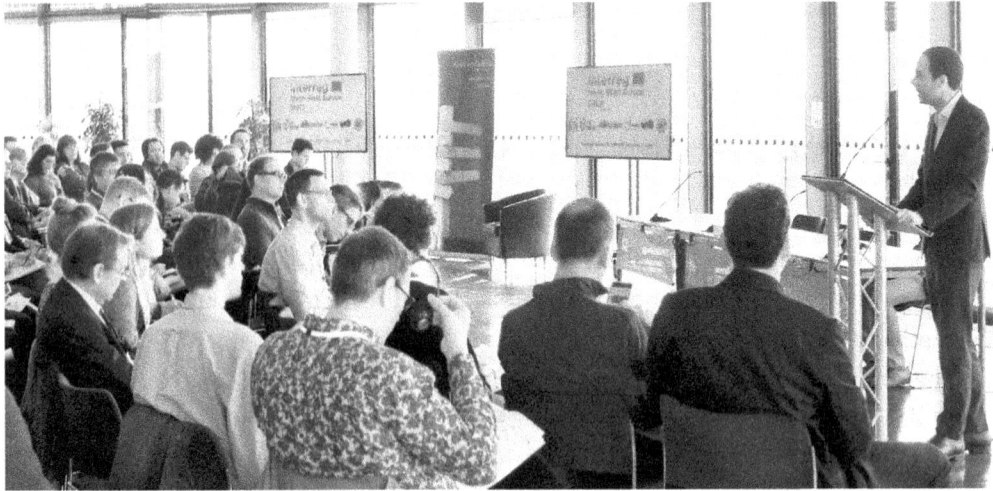

Fig 5.1. Second SHICC transnational event, London City Hall, 10 May 2019.

Europe discussed topics such as financing CLTs, how the CLT model can work for the most deprived, and how CLTs can promote resident involvement. A second major conference took place in London in May 2019. The final conference occurred in Brussels in June 2020, coinciding with a book launch for *On Common Ground* and a CLT symposium open to the general public.

Second, SHICC has provided resources to allow partners to inspire and to support other groups across the region of North-West Europe. Partners have been travelling across the region participating in reflections, presenting the CLT model, and coaching budding urban CLTs. In addition, a number of peer-to-peer exchanges have allowed established CLTs and recently formed groups to share their experiences and to learn from each other. Finally, the expansion of the National CLT Network of England and Wales' Start-Up Fund to serve the entire region is ongoing at the time of writing, with the first vouchers for technical expertise being handed out.

Third, SHICC has made new resources available for existing and future urban CLT projects. On the financial side, the first cross-regional analysis has been completed on urban CLTs' finance. This analysis provides information to interested groups on sources of funding for CLT development in France, England, Wales, Brussels, and Flanders, as well as possible funding at the European level. A measurement tool is currently being developed to evaluate the social impact of CLTs. This will be part of a broader set of tools that will help CLTs make their case to decision makers. Finally, the SHICC project will eventually produce a set of guides on how to set up a CLT, including a specific emphasis on managing the financial aspects of both the organization and its projects.

Last, but not least, the SHICC project has provided resources for four pioneering urban CLTs in London, Lille, Brussels, and Ghent to further consolidate their models, to document their progress, and to share their experience with the wider European CLT community. Papers will be delivered by the end of the project on various topics, including: community engagement, business planning, structuring deals with private and public funding, arrangements for the legal structure and governance of CLTs, and strategies for the scaling up of CLT operations.

The SHICC project may prove to have represented a watershed moment for the European CLT movement. By the project's end, it is anticipated that CLTs will have proven their value in dealing with the affordable housing crisis in Europe and will have become a true alternative for housing provision.

PATTERNS AND PROSPECTS FOR CLT DEVELOPMENT IN EUROPE

CLTs in Europe are structured and applied in many different ways and come in all shapes and sizes. Some are linked to a particular neighbourhood, while others cover an entire city, managing housing projects scattered across many areas. Some comprise only a few housing units, while others are part of larger housing developments and include dozens of units. CLTs also differ in their organization and operation, depending on whether they are initiated by municipal governments, communities, or local non-profits and depending on whether the national legislation authorizing them is more or less detailed in what a CLT is required to be.

Despite their differences, they all share a commitment to making permanently affordable housing a reality. This is why the notion of stewardship, be it through legal mechanisms or shared democratic governance, is central to the concept of a CLT. In addition, the inclusion of anti-speculative mechanisms is a key element of all CLTs, regardless of the resale formula that is used to calculate resale prices.

In the context of the SHICC project, a working definition of a CLT was put forward. SHICC's leaders believed this definition to encompass the majority of the region's urban CLTs:

> CLTs are non-profit, democratic, community-led organisations. They develop and manage homes that are affordable to low and median income households, as well as other assets that contribute to thriving local communities. They act as long-term stewards of these assets, ensuring they remain permanently affordable. This is achieved through mechanisms that ensure that any additional value generated is retained within the CLT.

Despite differences in terms of community involvement, ranging from the bottom-up approach of many English CLTs to the more top-down approach of the local authority-led French OFS model, all partners of the SHICC project have subscribed to this definition. It provides a common understanding and the common ground for all CLT initiatives in Europe.

Fig. 5.2. Informational brochure describing Sustainable Housing for Inclusive and Cohesive Cities, 2018. SHICC is a partnership of the Global Fund for Cities Development (FMDV), the National CLT Network of England and Wales, the City of Lille, CLT Ghent, London CLT, and CLT Brussels.

Prospects for Growth—and Potential Obstacles

Over the past ten years, the CLT has gained significant recognition in mainland Europe. Almost no one had heard of the model in 2008, but the CLT is now generally regarded as an attractive and effective strategy for tackling housing and urban problems.

The increasing acceptance of the CLT's approach to land stewardship and permanent affordability is primarily due to a worsening housing crisis across many countries. Living in many European cities is becoming more and more expensive; more and more people are no longer finding suitable and affordable housing. The construction of new social housing is in decline. Rising prices in market-priced housing make any subsidies available from government inadequate for low-income tenants who are trying to get into rental housing. The same is true for moderate-income households hoping to gain access to conventional forms of homeownership.

This mounting crisis in affordable housing is happening alongside problems of unsustainable urban growth, urban sprawl, and climate change, forcing governments to consider new policies and strategies for housing, land use, and urban development. At the same time, in recent years, there has been a widespread movement of citizens' initiatives, favouring a sharing economy and the Commons. There is widespread agreement on the need for new models.

All of this provided a fertile breeding ground for the new idea of European community land trusts. By focusing strongly on cooperation and cross-border exchanges from the start, the initiators of the first CLTs used this momentum to raise the CLTs' profile. Individuals in political circles, in the academic world, and in civil society, as well as activists in many citizen groups, got to know CLTs and started to see them as an interesting solution.

But setting up a community land trust is not the same as setting up a community garden. It requires a lot of money, a lot of expertise in various fields, and many adjustments to ensure that a CLT complies with a country's laws governing the ownership, leasing, and operation of real estate. For citizen activists who undertake a CLT initiative, it usually requires that they dare to take a cautious step towards cooperation with the government. Conversely, municipal governments who undertake a CLT initiative must dare to give more power to private citizens.

The flexibility of the model and the enthusiasm and perseverance of the first initiators ensured that the first hurdles to establishing a CLT and to developing CLT housing could be overcome. Hundreds of CLT homes, spread over a dozen cities, are currently in the process of being developed, mainly in England, Belgium and France. In other cities and in almost all European countries, groups are either exploring the formation of a CLT or already in the process of creating one.

Despite this great activity and attention, the CLT movement on the European mainland is still in its infancy. It remains an early and vulnerable phenomenon. The number of homes developed to date are a drop in the ocean, compared to the magnitude of the housing problem in many cities and countries. This movement will only be able to have a weighty and lasting impact if it becomes easier to set up CLTs and to develop permanently affordable homes. If every new organization and every new project is a marathon, impeded by countless hurdles, exhaustion will quickly set in.

Further growth will only be possible if European cooperation is continued and strengthened. Interesting building blocks are being developed in different cities, regions, and countries, which others will be able to use. For example, the success of CLT supporters in France, where the national government was persuaded to enact legislation authorizing *Organismes de Foncier Solidaire,* the French version of a CLT, and to create a new type of long-term ground lease, can inspire CLT activists in other countries. The fruitful cooperation that has developed in Brussels between a citizens' initiative and the government can serve as another example for citizens and cities that want to launch a CLT. The mortgage loans provided by the Brussels Housing Fund, moreover, can increase the confidence of lenders. Scholarly research, model contracts, and case studies of CLTs that are already in operation can be used to inform and to inspire new CLTs. The current European SHICC project has created a framework for lasting cross-national cooperation, which may help CLTs to gain access to more funding from the European Union, making it easier for CLTs to implement their projects.

It is too soon to say whether this young movement will succeed in playing a substantial role in addressing the housing crisis in European cities. But a foundation has been laid and a significant start has been made. In mainland Europe, the prospects look good for further growth and greater impact by CLTs in the coming years.

———

2021 POSTSCRIPT:
FURTHER GROWTH OF THE EUROPEAN CLT MOVEMENT

Joaquin de Santos

Despite the COVID pandemic and not being able to hold the international CLT conference that had been planned for 2020, the European community land trust movement has continued to grow and to spread. This short postscript aims to summarise recent developments in Europe that have occurred in the two years since our original essay was written.

Strengthening the European CLT Movement

The SHICC partnership has made a crucial contribution to supporting and growing the European CLT movement. The extension of the Start-up Fund has allowed 34 groups from across the North-West Europe zone to receive support at the initial stages of their CLT projects. It has also led to an upsurge of interest in the CLT model across the region. Tools and guides developed by the project have provided information and inspiration for these budding organizations and projects.[18]

This was not to be the final contribution of SHICC, however. This initiative had been due to conclude in September 2020, but obtained a one-year extension and integrated new partners, extending its reach. While continuing the work of strengthening existing pilots (including new areas of activity around the social economy and resident involvement), SHICC welcomed CLT champions from four new countries. Germany was represented by an organization named *id22*, which is supporting the establishment of a CLT in Berlin. The Netherlands was represented by *And the People*, which is supporting the establishment of a CLT in South East Amsterdam. Scotland was represented by *South of Scotland Community Housing* and Ireland was represented by *Self Organised Architecture*, with both organizations working to gain recognition of the CLT model within the context of their own countries.

In addition, the SHICC partnership has continued to work on expanding the financing for CLT projects. FMDV,[19] which has taken the lead in coordinating this work, has launched a feasibility study for the creation of a European financial intermediary for CLTs. Initial findings and recommendations are due by the Fall of 2021.

The success of SHICC has gained recognition at the EU level. In October 2020, SHICC won a prestigious *RegioStars Award* in the "Citizens Engagement for Cohesive European Cities" category, awarded to EU-funded projects that demonstrate excellence and new approaches in regional development. SHICC was one of five winners, out of 206 applications.

These developments have taken place amid the increasing prominence of affordable housing on the EU political agenda. The European Parliament has lately assumed a leading role in putting housing on the agenda by adopting a report on *Access to Decent and Affordable Housing for All*, drafted by Kim van Sparrentak MEP.[20] Notably this report:

Calls on the Commission, Member States and regional and local authorities to recognise, support and fund community-led, democratic, and collaborative housing solutions, including CLTs, as legitimate and viable means to provide housing . . .

The SHICC *EU CLT Policy Conference* that took place online in December 2020 illustrated this support, with policymakers and activists putting forward ideas for how CLTs can contribute to the European Union's policy agenda.[21]

Looking forward, SHICC project partners old and new got together to draft a Charter for the creation of an informal European CLT Network, which was adopted by all organisations in June 2021. It will guide the continuation of the work to foster the European CLT movement.

Recent CLT Developments in Selected Countries

Belgium. CLT Ghent (CLTG) has continued to work on its first project in the district of Meulestede. Construction is due to start early in 2022. Residents should be able to move into their CLT new homes by the beginning of 2023. In parallel, CLTG has collaborated with the City of Ghent and local organisations to open *SupermerKade*, a social grocery shop in the former offices of CLTG. The shop opened in April 2021, thus responding to a long-standing demand of the local community. In addition, CLTG started a second project on land provided by a private investor, where it will build two or three houses. This experiment could become an example for similar projects in Flanders. Finally, CLTG is investigating the possibility of renovating eight homes and renting them out to CLTG's candidates.[22]

As for Leuven, following the conclusion of the feasibility study, the City government and its partners have been pressing forward with establishment of a CLT. They have recruited a coordinator and launched a co-creation process that will involve all interested parties. Their aim is to set up the CLT's legal and governance structure by March 2022, and to carry out their first development on a plot of land near the train station.

The Flemish CLT coalition remains very active and is contributing to the spread of CLT projects across many other Flemish cities.

As for Wallonia, the SHICC Start-up Fund led to an upsurge of interest, with ten CLT projects supported through the scheme. These included a wide variety of projects in larger and smaller cities, driven by local groups, organisations, and public authorities. These projects include uses and spaces for activities other than housing. As a result, the Walloon

CLT coalition has gained a new impetus and is advocating for a study to continue disseminating the model in the region.

France.[23]At present, fifteen families have successfully moved into the first OFS homes in Lille, and more than 100 homes are under development in seven projects across the city. At the national level, 64 OFS entities are now established. Half of them are part of the national network, *Foncier Solidaire France*, that was informally launched in Lille in 2018 and formally incorporated in early 2021. In addition, a new category of actors has joined the OFS movement: social housing organisations — i.e. public or private companies that act in the general interest by building and managing low-income rental and ownership housing. Since 2018, a national law has enabled them to be recognised as an OFS. This allows them to produce and to manage OFS homes alongside their main activities, which remain within the same framework as before.

The Netherlands.[24] The effort to create a CLT in the Bijlmer district in Southeast Amsterdam, a huge modernist high-rise housing complex constructed for urban renewal in the 1960s and 1970s with mainly social housing, has pressed forward thanks to the efforts of *And the People* and support from the City of Amsterdam. In June 2021, the original community-based planning committee became an open neighbourhood association, *CLT H-Buurt,* with over 140 members. *And The People* has continued to support this local planning process in terms of capacity building, and has organised expert coalitions to perform multiple forms of action research. This research is designed to link the benefits of the CLT model to municipal policies and the reality of urban development through participatory processes and learning by doing in order to build coalitions and communities around the CLT model in Amsterdam.A further elaboration has been made to explore how self-building practices and policies might be incorporated into the legal, financial, and governance aspects of *CLT H-Buurt*. In addition, local actors have developed an innovative approach that links the CLT model to the "doughnut economy" framework of Kate Raworth, which the municipality of Amsterdam has adopted to ensure that the growth of the city remains within planetary and societal boundaries. CLT activists are now advocating for the inclusion of "doughnut" criteria in public tenders whereby the City of Amsterdam makes public assets available (under certain conditions) for cooperative housing projects. *CLT H-Buurt* hopes this will provide an opportunity to develop a first project, which can serve as a pilot case to scale up the CLT model to other neighbourhoods and cities.

Germany.[25] Berlin's *Stadtbodenstiftung* (the German name for a CLT) is now officially recognized as a non-profit foundation. To date, about 150 private donors have contributed 160,000 Euros for the organization's initial capitalization and the Berlin Senate

Department for Urban Development and Housing is assisting with start-up funding. The first projects to be developed will likely entail the *Stadtbodenstiftung* acquiring land from socially minded private owners of multi-unit apartment buildings. A housing cooperative would then buy each building and sign a long-term lease with the *Stadtbodenstiftung* for the underlying land.

Spain.[26] CLT discussions in Barcelona have made great progress. The municipal government aims to more than double the number of affordable housing units in the city, primarily by investing in the construction of publicly owned rental housing and by collaborating with private, limited- and non-profit affordable housing providers. The City will be making public land available to the latter.

In order to overcome the negative effects of competitive public tenders for this land, the Barcelona City Council took inspiration from the CLT model. In December 2020, a Collaboration Agreement was launched between the City and cooperative and non-profit affordable housing providers. Through this Agreement, the partners will propose one project per available plot to the City and the Federation of Social Housing Developers (GHS), who will then evaluate those proposals, following transparent principles. The City and the project's developer will then sign a long-term lease for the land.

The objective of this Collaboration Agreement is to deliver 1,000 affordable housing units in the next years, while strengthening the emerging local non-profit and cooperative housing sector. The next step will be to explore how residents can be included in the Agreement on an equal footing with the housing providers, in order to become fully-fledged CLTs.

The CLT model is progressing elsewhere in Spain too. An adaptation of the CLT model to the Spanish context looks promising. It aims at creating an alternative land regime for a first "micro city" [*microkosmos* project] that includes the rehabilitation and reuse of derelict rural buildings and the revitalization of rural and forest land through eco-systemic development. In addition, over the past few years the Legal Lab on Evictions [*Laboratorio Jurídico sobre Desahucios*] at Cordoba University has conducted research on the CLT and other collective forms of tenure, developing legal alternatives and playing an advisory role in Spain and beyond.

Portugal.[27] As a result of advocacy and information work, a small group of CLT advisors is emerging in Portugal, primarily engaged in the Lisbon Metropolitan Area. This has resulted in meetings with cooperative movements and neighbourhoods associations who are on the frontline to support those excluded from housing and those suffering evictions. It seems that a large piece of land called "Talude," cultivated for years by organised families mostly of Cabo Verdean origin who live there, could become the country's first CLT. This would bring security of tenure, putting an end to evictions and threats.

Scotland.[28] Scotland's pioneering urban community-led regeneration project, the Mid-steeple Quarter project, has progressed to Phase One. Centered on redevelopment of "The Oven" building, this project would produce seven affordable accommodations, as well as creative enterprise space on the ground floor.

The community-led housing sector welcomed the Scottish Government's recent *Housing to 2040* strategy report. This report proposed exploring an urban variant of the Rural Housing Fund (£30 million), as well as committing £325m for a place-based investment programme supporting mixed-use regeneration that will make progress towards a target of 100,000 affordable homes by 2032.

In the wider community ownership context, the Scottish Government introduced new Right to Buy legislation in 2020 which extended the right of communities to acquire public assets when used to further sustainable development.[29] The urban community ownership movement continues to grow, with Community Land Scotland reporting in March 2021 that 20% of all community-owned assets are now in towns and cities, supported by the Scottish Land Fund — which Parliament has committed to double (to £20 million) by the end of term.

Ireland.[30] The Affordable Housing Act of 2021 was passed by Parliament and signed into law in July 2021. It references the Community Land Trust, which is the first recognition in law (and policy) of the CLT in Ireland. The amendment for the CLT's inclusion received cross-party support. Several nascent CLTs are currently in development and an innovative Threefold Community Asset Trust (TCAT) is being established in County Kilkenny, which will incorporate housing (including for people with support needs), organic cultivation, and arts/cultural projects.

Looking Ahead: Continuing The Growth of the European CLT Movement Through Collaboration

There have been significant developments both at the European level and in individual countries since our original chapter was written for *On Common Ground*. The seeds planted by the pioneering CLT projects in England, Belgium, and France have spread within these countries and across other geographies in the region thanks to the collaborative work of the SHICC partnership and the tireless advocacy of national champions and networks. Mutual learning and exchange, and the provision of expertise for budding CLT projects, have been a key to nurturing this growth.

However, many CLT projects are at early stages of development and might still encounter significant obstacles throughout their journey. In addition, the conclusion of the SHICC project in September 2021 means that these resources will no longer be available for European collaboration among CLTs. But the European CLT movement is working hard on identifying new sources of support in order to continue the collaboration that has been so successful in spreading the CLT model across Europe. The creation of an informal European CLT network is a first step in this direction.

Notes

1. Audrey Linkenheld is Local Councillor for Innovation and Social Mix, City of Lille, and Secretary of Organisme de Foncier Solidaire of the Lille European Metropolis.

2. OFS was made a part of national housing law (ALUR law).

3. This was made possible thanks to very long-term (60-80 years) loans by Banque des Territoires, enabling OFSs to buy land.

4. Further avenues for expanding the OFS model are currently being explored. They include the resale of social housing, the fight against precarious housing, and irregular settlments.

5. Marc Neelen, Jip Nelissen, and Rense Bos contributed to this profile of CLT developments in The Netherlands.

6. Their interest in the CLT was piqued through various exchanges with CLT Brussels and by the participation of City in the Making in European CLT meetings.

7. Michael LaFond contributed to this profile of CLT developments in Germany.

8. The description of Ex-Rotaprint by one of the artists who led the campaign to acquire this former industrial site is remarkably similar to how most CLT leaseholders would describe their own form of tenure: "We have a 99-year, inheritable building rights contract with the foundations, meaning we pay them an annual lease for the ground. We then own the buildings and can work with them without having to ask for anything. The only—very important—condition is that we can't sell the compound because they [i.e., the two foundations] own the ground" (*http://www.uncubemagazine.com/blog/16598237*).

9. Matteo Robiglio contributed to this profile of CLT developments in Italy.

10. The event was part of *We-Traders,* a travelling exhibition on new forms of economy in Europe.

11. Cyril Royez contributed to this profile of CLT developments in Switzerland.

12. Yves Cabannes contributed to this profile of CLT interest in Spain and Portugal.

13. Authored by Linsay Chalmers and Mike Staples, with the assistance of Dr. Calum McLeod.

14. Land Reform Act 2003 (Scotland), followed by Land Reform Act 2016 (Scotland).

15. Community Empowerment Act 2015 (Scotland).

16. In 2017, the Scottish Government set up a Scottish Land Commission to drive forward land reform. Key aspects of the Commission's work are aimed at bringing community landownership into the mainstream and making effective use of land for the common good.

17. This profile of CLT interest in Ireland was authored by Tom O'Donnell.

18. Available at *https://www.nweurope.eu/projects/project-search/shicc-sustainable-housing-for-inclusive-and-cohesive-cities/#tab-5*

19. FMDV (Global Fund for Cities' Development) is a global network of local and regional governments with the mission to develop and promote investment and financing solutions for urban development. Both a network of expertise and an incubator for operational strategies, FMDV is an instrument for technical assistance and financial engineering and promotes a holistic approach to financing, working at all levels of intervention and with all the actors.

20. Full report here: *https://www.europarl.europa.eu/doceo/document/TA-9-2021-0020_EN.pdf*

21. Watch here : *https://www.youtube.com/watch?v=oDq_I6LZhz0*

22. Update on the CLT Ghent contributed by Frank Vandepitte.

23. Update contributed by Audrey Linkenheld, 1st Deputy Mayor for Ecological Transition and Sustainable Development at the City of Lille, and sponsor of the legislation that created the OFS model during her time in the French parliament.

24. Update contributed by Jip Nelissen and Joris Kramer. For resources see: *www.clthbuurt.nl* / *www.clt.amsterdam* / *www.cooperate.eco*

25. Update contributed by Michael LaFond.

26. Update contributed by Eduard Cabré Romans and Yves Cabannes.

27. Update contributed by Yves Cabannes.

28. Update contributed by Mike Staples and Annabel Pidgeon.

29. Right to Buy Land to Further Sustainable Development — *Part 5* of the Land Reform (Scotland) Act 2016 .

30. Update contributed by Tom O'Donnell.

ABOUT THE CONTRIBUTORS

NELE AERNOUTS is an architect, urban designer, and researcher. She is a postdoctoral researcher at Cosmopolis and teaches in the MSc in Urban Design and Spatial Planning (SteR*) at the Vrije Universiteit Brussel. Her research interests include collective housing, social housing, and participatory planning, with a specific focus on underprivileged groups. During her PhD, she studied diverse forms of housing commons and land tenures in the Brussels Capital Region, such as community land trusts and housing cooperatives, focusing on spatial and participatory dimensions. Currently she coordinates a LivingLab project tackling the regeneration of large-scale social estates.

LINE ALGOED is a PhD researcher at Cosmopolis, Center for Urban Research at the Vrije Universiteit in Brussels and a Research Fellow at the International Institute of Social Studies in The Hague. She works with the Caño Martín Peña CLT in Puerto Rico on international exchanges among communities involved in land struggles. She is also Vice President of the Center for CLT Innovation. Previously, Line was a World Habitat Awards Program Manager at BSHF (now World Habitat). She holds an MA in Cultural Anthropology from the University of Leiden and an MA in Sociology from the London School of Economics.

TOM ARCHER, PhD, is a Research Fellow at Sheffield Hallam University, specialising in housing and community development. Between 2010 – 2016, he was one of the National CLT Network's Technical Advisors, providing support to urban CLTs in England. Tom's doctoral research focused on the factors affecting housing collectivism in England and Canada, and its costs and benefits. Tom has led major evaluations of community-led housing programmes, alongside other large housing market studies. He has co-authored influential reports on the private housebuilding industry in the UK, and the growth of community-owned assets.

YVES CABANNES (y.cabannes@ucl.ac.uk) is an urban specialist, activist and scholar. Over the past forty years he has been involved in research and development on urban issues, people-led initiatives, and local democracy with NGOs and local governments in

Asia, Latin America, Africa and the Middle East. Since the early 1990s, he has supported, researched, taught, and advocated for participatory budgeting and planning, urban agriculture, community land trusts, and housing rights in different regions of the world and has published widely on these topics. He became Emeritus Professor of Development Planning at the University College London/Development Planning Unit in 2015.

TOM CHANCE is the Chief Executive of the National CLT Network for England and Wales and leads on its strategy, public policy and advocacy work, and building relationships with industry bodies. Before this, he worked in London's City Hall as head of office for the Green Party Group on the London Assembly. That's where got the CLT bug, helping the London CLT to secure its first development opportunity. He has also worked for a sustainable construction company, and as a consultant for clients such as World Habitat, a grouping of UK Parliamentarians, and various local councils.

JOHN EMMEUS DAVIS is a founding partner of Burlington Associates in Community Development, a national consulting cooperative. He was housing director in Burlington, Vermont under Mayors Bernie Sanders and Peter Clavelle. Community land trusts have been a prominent part of his professional practice and scholarly writing for nearly 40 years. His publications include *Contested Ground* (1991), *The Affordable City* (1994), *The City-CLT Partnership* (2008), *The Community Land Trust Reader* (2010), and *Manuel d'antispéculation immobilière* (2014). He co-produced the film, *Arc of Justice,* and currently serves as President of the Center for CLT Innovation (*https://cltweb.org*). He holds an MS and PhD from Cornell University.

GEERT DE PAUW has been active for more than 20 years championing the right to housing in Brussels as an activist and community worker. In 2008, following a study visit to the Champlain Housing Trust, he began advocating for the establishment of a CLT in Brussels. He coordinated the CLT feasibility study that was commissioned by the Brussels Capital Region. He has been a coordinator of the CLT Brussels since 2012. He was also a co-founder of SHICC (Sustainable Housing for Inclusive and Cohesive Cities), a European partnership whose goal is to create a thriving CLT movement in Europe.

JOAQUÍN DE SANTOS studied political science and European politics in Switzerland, the UK, France and Belgium. After working in European affairs and on industrial heritage projects for seven years, he joined the staff of the CLT Brussels in early 2018 to coordinate the European project, Sustainable Housing for Inclusive and Cohesive Cities (SHICC). He has had a long-standing interest in urban struggles for the right to the city and industrial and social heritage. In his spare time, he is pursuing a PhD in urban policy at the University of Antwerp, Belgium.

ELISA FERREIRA has been the European Commissioner for Cohesion and Reforms since December 2019, in charge of the European Union's cohesion policies and support for national reforms. Before that, she was Vice-Governor of the Bank of Portugal (2017 – 2019) and a Member of the European Parliament (2004 – 2016), working on a number of financial regulation dossiers. She previously served as Portugal's Minister for Planning (1999 – 2002) and Minister for the Environment (1995 – 1999). She holds a degree in Economics from the University of Porto and a Ph.D. from the University of Reading.

CALUM GREEN worked with the London CLT in various roles over a ten-year period starting in 2011. Most recently, he served as Communities & Campaigns Director (2015 – 2019) and as Chief Executive (2019 – 2021). In August 2021, he accepted a new position as Director of Advocacy and Communications at Involve, the UK's leading public participation organisation, where he is working to ensure that decisions are made by those they most affect. He remains involved with the London CLT as a local member in his neighbourhood of Peckham in south London.

CATHERINE HARRINGTON is co-Chief Executive of the National CLT Network (*http:// www.communitylandtrusts.org.uk*) in England and Wales, having founded the organisation in September 2010. Catherine joined the Network from the Ministry for Housing, Communities and Local Government. Previously she worked at the Notting Hill Housing Trust and the Institute for Public Policy Research. In 2017, she received the Swann-Matthei Award from Grounded Solutions in the USA, recognizing her many contributions to the CLT movement. Catherine has an MSc in City Design and Social Science from the London School of Economics and holds a BA Hons in Social Anthropology from the University of Cambridge.

MARÍA E. HERNÁNDEZ-TORRALES holds an LLM in environmental law from the Vermont Law School and an MA in Business Education from New York University. She studied for her undergraduate and Juris Doctor degrees at the University of Puerto Rico. Since 2005 she has been doing pro bono legal work for the Proyecto ENLACE and for the Fideicomiso de la Tierra del Caño Martín Peña. Since 2008, Hernández-Torrales has worked as an attorney and clinical professor at the University of Puerto Rico School of Law where she teaches the Community Economic Development Clinic.

STEPHEN HILL (smdhill@gmail.com) is an independent public interest practitioner in planning and housing development, advising central and local governments, developers, housing associations, and community housing groups. In 2014, he visited the USA and Canada as a Churchill Fellow, reporting on approaches to the co-production of housing and neighbourhood development by the "state" and citizens through community organising. He recently retired as trustee of the National CLT Nework (for England and Wales) and Chair of the UK Cohousing Network. In 2017, he received the "John Emmeus Davis Award for Scholarship" from Grounded Solutions, and has a lovely wizard's hat to prove it.

PHILIP ROSS (rosspe97@gmail.com) is the former Mayor of Letchworth Garden City and is the current Chairman of the New Garden Cities Alliance, an organization that champions the social goals of the Garden City Movement. He is an international speaker on Garden Cities and, together with Yves Cabannes, wrote the book *21st Century Garden Cities of To-Morrow — A Manifesto*. He still lives in Letchworth and is married with three children. He works as a freelance business analyst.

DAVE SMITH is a community organizer and affordable housing practitioner based in London, England. From 2008–2014, he served as the founding Executive Director of the London Community Land Trust, which is now the largest CLT in the UK. Prior to this, Dave worked for the British Council and on Barack Obama's 2008 primary and presidential election campaigns. More recently, he has worked at the National Housing Federation, CDS Co-operatives and is currently Head of Community Engagement at Eastlight Community Homes. He holds degrees from King's College, the University of Cambridge, and The Bartlett School of Planning, University College London.

www.ingramcontent.com/pod-product-compliance
Lightning Source LLC
Chambersburg PA
CBHW080558030426
42336CB00019B/3244